W

# Prereq[illegible]kills

Students will need to know how to add, subtract, multiply, and divide to be successful with this book. Not there yet? Don't worry, we have workbooks that focus on these skills.

# Learning Goals

- Read and understand word problems.
- Identify the question and what it's asking.
- Distinguish what information is needed.
- Create an equation.
- Solve the problem.

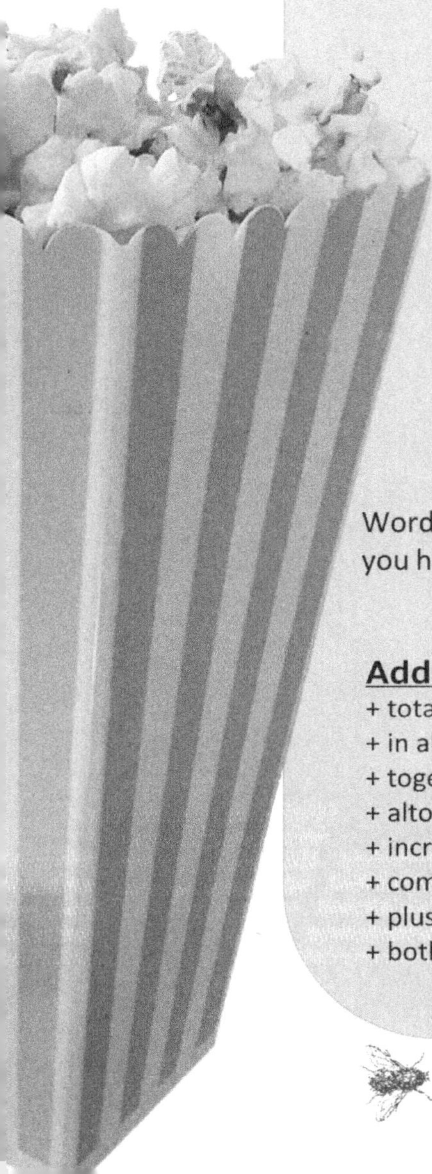

# Helpful Strategies

1. Underline the question.
2. Use "**keywords**" to decide what the question is asking.
3. Circle important information.
4. Remember that some information may not be needed.
5. Make an equation and solve it.
6. Check your answer. Does your answer make sense?

# Common Keywords

Words and phrases can help you decide which operation to use, but you have to pay attention to how these words are used in the sentence.

| Addition: | Subtraction: | Multiplication: | Division |
|---|---|---|---|
| + total | – left | x total | ÷ per |
| + in all | – fewer | x in all | ÷ half |
| + together | – take away | x triple | ÷ parts |
| + altogether | – how many more | x double | ÷ separated |
| + increased by | – difference | x increased by | ÷ shared equally |
| + combined | – decrease | x every | ÷ equal amounts |
| + plus | – minus | x times | ÷ divided |
| + both | – less | x by | ÷ each |

Name: ____________________

Score:

① A tower on the king's castle was the tallest tower in the land, until a queen in a neighboring kingdom built a tower that was 9 meters taller. If the queen's new tower is 44 meters tall, how tall is the king's tower?

② The king was jealous and immediately ordered his tower to be built 12 meters taller than its current height. The builders estimate that every 1 meter of height added to the tower will require 145 additional stones. If each stone costs 4 silver coins, how much should the builders tell the king the estimated stones will cost?

③ The king paid 68 silver coins to buy wagons to move the stones, and another 275 silver coins to hire workers to load the stones onto the wagons and transport the stones to his castle. How many silver coins is that all together?

④ The king wants all the stones transported within the next 4 days. If the workers still need to transport 560 stones, on average, how many stones do they need to transport each day?

⑤ When the neighboring queen heard about the king's construction project, she decided to give the king some bags of cement that had been left over after building her own tower. The king had purchased 157 bags of cement and received 35 more bags of cement from the queen. How many bags of cement does the king have now?

⑥ Touched by the queen's kind act, the king commanded his servants to hold a grandiose celebration for both his servants and the queen's servants, and he wanted his royal chef to have a meal prepared for each of the servants. If the queen has 957 servants and the king has 834 servants, how many meals should the royal chef prepare?

**Facts:**

- **Lightning bolts can strike multiple locations at once.**
- **One bolt can contain a billion volts of electricity.**

Name: ______________________

Score:

1. If a lightning bolt heats the air it passes through to 24,000 °C and the surface of the sun is about 6,000 °C, how many times hotter is the lightning than the sun's surface?

2. One lightning bolt contained 472 million volts of electricity. A second bolt had 259 million volts. How many volts did they have together?

3. Only about 10 percent of people struck by lightning die of it. That means if 100 people are struck, 10 of those people would likely die. If true, how many would survive?

**Facts:**

- **Most who are struck by lightning survive, but many will have lifelong damage from the strike.**
- **Lightning strikes can cause severe burns that damage tissues inside and outside the body.**

4. The bright flash of light from lightning travels at the speed of light, which is about 186,000 miles per second. The sound of thunder travels at the speed of sound, which is about 1 mile in 5 seconds. So, which is faster, the speed of light or the speed of sound?

5. Since it takes sound about 5 seconds to travel a mile, you can estimate how far away a lightning bolt is from you. Once you see a lightning flash, start counting. The bolt is one additional mile from you for every 5 seconds that pass before hearing the thunder. Knowing this, how far away is a lightning bolt if it takes the thunder 15 seconds to reach you after the flash?

**Facts:**

- **Bolts can strike over 20 miles away from a storm.**
- **They are called a "bolt from the blue" because the sky is often blue with no sign of storms or danger.**

6. Lightning likes to strike tall objects. The Empire State Building gets struck a lot. If it was struck 44 times last year and 56 times the year before that, how many times was it struck in those two years combined?

**Trivia:**

- **What is the study of lightning called?**

Name: ____________________

Score:

① Levi and Mel went fishing two days in a row. The first day, they caught 8 fish. The next day, they caught 40 fish. How many times more fish did they catch the second day than the first?

② Of the 40 fish they caught the second day, they released 27 of the fish back into the water. How many fish did they keep the second day?

③ Levi and Mel each brought a can of worms to use as bait. Levi's can had 33 worms and Mel's can had 29 worms. By the end of their fishing trip, there were only 6 worms left. How many worms did they use while fishing?

④ Of the 48 fish they caught, 6 were catfish, 8 were bass, and the rest were bluegills. How many bluegills did they catch?

⑤ The largest catfish they caught was 9 pounds 5 ounces. The largest bass they caught was 3 pounds 8 ounces. How much heavier was their largest catfish than their largest bass? (Hint: There are 16 ounces in a pound.)

⑥ Mel wanted to buy a new fishing rod that costs 30 pounds and 15 more fishhooks that costs a pound for every 5 fishhooks. How much will it cost to buy the fishing rod and 15 fishhooks?

Name: ______________________

Score:

**Facts:**

- **The Moon is Earth's only natural satellite.**
- **It takes the Moon about 27 days to orbit the Earth.**
- **Earth's gravity is about 6 times stronger than the Moon's.**

1. The Earth has a diameter of about 12,741 km. The Moon's diameter is about 3,473 km. How much wider is Earth's diameter?

2. The distance between the Earth and the Moon is about 384,400 km. Write that distance in word form.

3. Scientists worried that the first astronauts to land on the Moon might bring germs from outer space back to Earth. So, these astronauts were placed in quarantine for 3 weeks when they returned from space. How many days of quarantine is that?

21

**Facts:**

- **The Moon's atmosphere is incredibly thin, so there is no wind to blow astronaut footprints away.**
- **One Earth day is about 24 hours long, but one "Moon day" is about 29 and a half days long.**
- **A Moon day has about 2 Earth weeks of sunlight (daytime) and two Earth weeks of darkness (nighttime).**

4. Daytime temperatures on the Moon's equator can be 121 °C, while nighttime temperatures can be -134 °C. How much cooler is this nighttime temperature than the daytime temperature?

155 °C

5. The Moon's coldest temperatures are in crater shadows at its poles. Using infrared tools, NASA found that the temperature in one crater's shadow was –245 °C. How much colder is that than 121 °C?

366 °C

6. The weight of an object on the Moon would be about 6 times heavier if it were brought to Earth. If a rock weighs 40 grams on the Moon, how much would it weigh on Earth?

***Just for fun*:**
*If you went to the Moon, you would be 6 times lighter. How much would you weigh on the Moon?*

**Trivia:**

- **NASA used radio transmitters to communicate with Apollo astronauts. How long does it take radio waves to travel from the Earth to the Moon?**

Name: ____________________

Score:

① Rocky is going to the airport to pick up his brother Leo. On his way, he remembered that Leo loves to eat BLT sandwiches. He decided to buy 2 cups of coffee and 4 BLT sandwiches. If a cup of coffee costs £3 and a BLT sandwich costs £4, how much will Rocky need to pay in all?

£22

② Rocky arrived at the airport at 11:15 AM and immediately received a text message from his brother Leo. Leo was texting to let Rocky know that his flight was delayed due to poor weather conditions, and that it will be another 2 hours and 30 minutes before his plane arrives. If Leo's estimate is correct, what time should his flight arrive at the airport?

1:45 Pm

③ Rocky played a video game on his phone while waiting for Leo's airplane to arrive. If each of the game's matches takes 15 minutes, how long would it take him to finish playing 8 matches?

2 hr

④ Leo finally arrived at the airport with 2 large luggage bags. If one bag weighed 37 pounds and the other bag weighed 38 pounds, how much did the bags weigh together?

75 pounds

⑤ Before heading home, Leo and Rocky decided to buy some souvenirs for their mother who was waiting for them. Since they know she is a book lover, they bought 3 books that cost £13.99 each. If the cashier gave Leo £8.03 worth of change, how much had Leo originally given the cashier for the books?

50 pounds

⑥ On their way home, Rocky realized his car's fuel tank was low and decided to fill it up. If his car's fuel tank can hold 50 liters and there were only 6 liters of fuel left, how much would Rocky need to pay to fill the fuel tank, when the price of fuel at the station is £1.38 per liter?

60.72

Name: ____________________

Score:

**Facts:**

- **The world's smallest birds are hummingbirds.**
- **There are more than 300 species of hummingbirds.**

① The bee hummingbird is often 5 cm long and frequently mistaken for a bee while flying. Which battery represents a bee hummingbird's length?

The 14mm by 50 mm battery

② The giant hummingbird is the largest hummingbird species. It's about 20 cm long. How many times longer is that than a bee hummingbird?

4

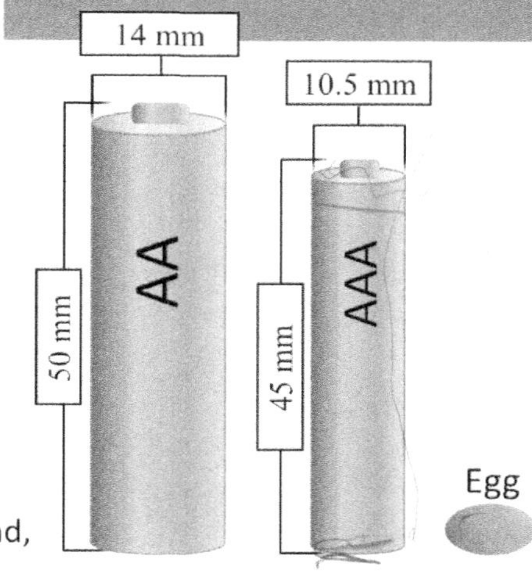


③ The diameter (width) of an AAA battery is roughly the length of the smallest hummingbird eggs. How long is that? 10.5 mm

④ If a hummingbird can flap its wings 70 times a second, how many times can its wings flap in 8 seconds?

560

**Facts:**

- **They are the only birds that can fly backward.**
- **Hummingbirds often flap their wings 70 times per second, which creates a "humming" noise.**
- **All this wing flapping uses a lot of energy, so hummingbirds spend most of their day eating.**
- **They can pollinate over 1,000 flowers a day.**

⑤ One hummingbird ate nectar from 1,248 flowers yesterday. If it had spent 8 hours eating nectar yesterday, on average, how many flowers did it eat from each hour?

156 ~~115~~ flowers

⑥ Most ruby-throated hummingbirds fly south for the winter. Many travel 500 miles across the Gulf of Mexico without stopping to rest. If a hummingbird flies 25 miles per hour, how long would it take to cross the Gulf of Mexico?

16 hours

**Trivia:**

- **How fast does a hummingbird's heart beat?**

Name: ____________________

Score:

① Mica and many of his family members are visiting a zoo to celebrate his grandmother's birthday. The zoo's entrance fee is £7 for each child and £9 for each adult. If his family has a total of 12 people who need to enter, of which 5 are kids, how much will Mica's family need to pay?

② Mica's family wants to feed some of the zoo's birds. They have already spent a lot of money to enter the zoo, so they decided that they will only buy £12 worth of bird food. If each pack of bird food costs £1.50, how many packs can they buy with £12?

③ A zookeeper mentioned that the zoo's 3 leopards usually eat 420 pounds of meat each week. On average, how many pounds of meat is that for each leopard per day?

④ The zoo has trained parrots. These parrots perform in a show 5 times a day. If the auditorium is large enough for 420 people to attend each of the shows, how many people could attend the show each day?

⑤ Mica's family met a zookeeper holding a brownish-yellow snake. The zookeeper explained that it is a 7-foot-long rat snake. She also mentioned that the longest snake in the zoo is a reticulated python, and that it is 3 times longer than the rat snake. How long is the zoo's reticulated python?

⑥ A zookeeper needs to inspect and clean each foot of every camel. If the zoo has 13 camels, how many camel feet will the zookeeper need to inspect and clean?

Name: ____________________

Score:

## Facts:

- Pure gold is soft, easy to bend, and easy to scratch.
- That's why pure gold is not used for jewelry. Other metals are mixed with the gold to make it stronger.

① The biggest gold coin was made by Australia's Perth Mint. It weighs about 2,204 pounds and it's about 80 cm wide and 12 cm thick. How many more cm wide is it than thick?

14k indicates 14 karat gold.

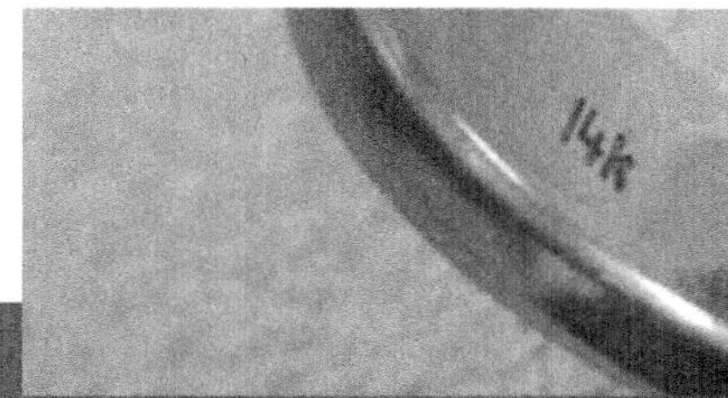


② Large amounts of gold are often stored as bricks. If one brick weighs about 12 kg, how much would 9 bricks weigh?

③ According to the US Mint, Fort Knox held about 147.3 million ounces of gold in the year 2020. But in 1941, it had 649.6 million ounces. How much more gold did Fort Knox hold in 1941?

## Facts:

- Gold is used in electronics because it's a great electrical conductor and doesn't tarnish or rust.
- Only silver and copper conduct electricity better.
- A cellphone has about 50 pence of gold inside. Computers, TV's, and radios contain gold too.
- Satellites use gold plating and circuits because silver and copper quickly tarnish in outer space.

④ The US Mint also claimed to hold about 2.7 million ounces of gold at Working Stock, 43.8 million ounces in Denver, and 54 million ounces at West Point. How much gold did all three locations hold together?

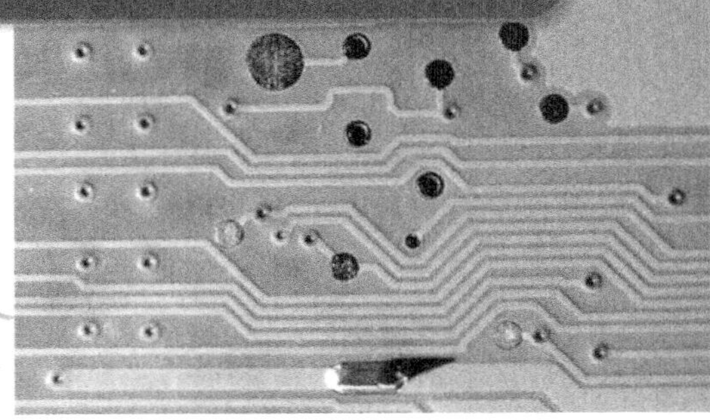

⑤ A miner found 17 gold nuggets one month and 25 nuggets the next. If she sold 23 of these nuggets, how many does she have left?

⑥ Six treasure hunters found two old shipwrecks. They recovered 537 gold coins from the first ship and 1,601 gold coins from the second ship. If these treasure hunters each keep an equal number of coins and donate the remainders, how many coins will each treasure hunter get and how many will they donate?

## Trivia:

- Why do people bite gold?

Name: ____________________

Score:

(1) There are 25 history books, 36 mathematics books, 16 English books, and 9 philosophy books in the school library. How many times more mathematics books does the library have than philosophy books?

(2) There were 6,127 fiction books in the library but 231 were transferred to another library and 17 were never returned. How many fiction books are left?

(3) Ryan reads 20 pages each day. At this rate, how long would it take him to finish a story that is 380 pages long?

(4) Marc loves to read mystery books and Ella likes comic books. If Marc finishes 3 books every 6 days and Ella finishes 4 books every 5 days, how many books will they read in 30 days combined?

(5) There are 15 shelves of books available in the Circulation Section of the library. If each shelf contains 50 books, how many books are there in the Circulation Section?

(6) Once books are returned to the library, the librarian needs to put them back in their correct locations on the bookshelves. If the librarian can put 4 books back per minute. How long would it take him to finish putting away 1,376 books into their correct locations on the shelves?

Name: ____________

Score:

**Facts:**

- **Native Central Americans probably invented chocolate about 4,000 years ago.**
- **For most of history, chocolate was a bitter drink.**

① The first solid chocolate bar was invented in 1847. Milk chocolate was invented in about 1865. How many years later was milk chocolate invented?

② It takes about 400 cacao beans to make a pound of chocolate. If a cacao tree produces 2,400 cacao beans, how many pounds of chocolate can be made from its beans?
**(*Hint: It may help to skip count by 400.*)**

**Facts:**

- **Montezuma, an Aztec ruler, loved chocolate, allegedly drinking 50 goblets of it each day.**
- **The Aztecs used cacao beans as a currency.**
- **Spanish explorers didn't like the bitter taste of chocolate and were the first to add sugar to it.**

③ If an Aztec blanket used to cost 80 cacao beans and a bowl used to cost 35 cacao beans, how much would 2 blankets and 4 bowls have cost?

④ An English pirate ship captured a Spanish ship carrying cacao beans before most English people knew what chocolate was. The pirates thought the beans were dried sheep poop, so they burned them with the ship. If this ship had carried 8 bags of cacao beans and each bag was worth 9 gold coins, how many gold coins worth of cacao did the pirates destroy?

**Facts:**

- **Chocolate usually contains fragments of insects.**
- **Despite the previous fact, billions of kg of chocolate are still eaten every year, and often given as gifts to loved ones.**

⑤ If 67 million pounds of chocolate were sold on Valentine's Day last year and 64 million pounds the year before, how many pounds were sold in both years combined?

⑥ The U.S. Food and Drug Administration allows chocolate to have up to an average of 60 insect fragments for every 100 grams of chocolate. Would 35 insect fragments in 50 grams be allowed? *Explain why or why not.*

**Trivia:**

- **What is "dark chocolate"?**

Name: ____________________

Score:

(1) Dr. Lee, a dentist, has a bunch of patients in her clinic Monday morning. Emy, Carl, and Patricia are scheduled for tooth extraction, Mico and Holly are scheduled for teeth whitening, and Joel is scheduled for a dental implant. If tooth extraction, teeth whitening, and dental implant cost £90, £40, and £179 respectively, how much money would Dr. Lee collect from these patients?

(2) One of Miriam's molars is infected. She's currently in a lot of pain. Dr. Lee says the best thing to do is have the tooth extracted. A tooth extraction is normally £90 but Miriam brought a £12 off coupon with her. If Miriam uses the coupon, how much would her tooth extraction cost?

(3) Dr. Lee ordered 1,400 toothbrushes to give to her clients. Three months later, she only had 438 toothbrushes left. How many toothbrushes did she give away?

(4) If a teeth whitening procedure takes 45 minutes, how many procedures can be done in 6 consecutive hours?

(5) The monthly revenue of Dr. Lee's dental clinic is £75,000 but some of this money will be used to pay for utilities and taxes. If the electricity bill is £510, the water bill is £350, the telephone bill is £145, and the clinic's business tax is £8,400, how much will these utilities and taxes cost all together?

(6) Dr. Lee has 4 dental hygienists working in the clinic. If each dental hygienist is paid £35 per hour and they work 8 hours a day, how much money does the clinic spend each day for its dental hygienists combined?

Name: ____________________

Score:

**Facts:**

- **Sea turtles spend most of their life at sea but return to land to dig a nest and lay a clutch of eggs.**
- **A sea turtle clutch can have 100 or more eggs.**

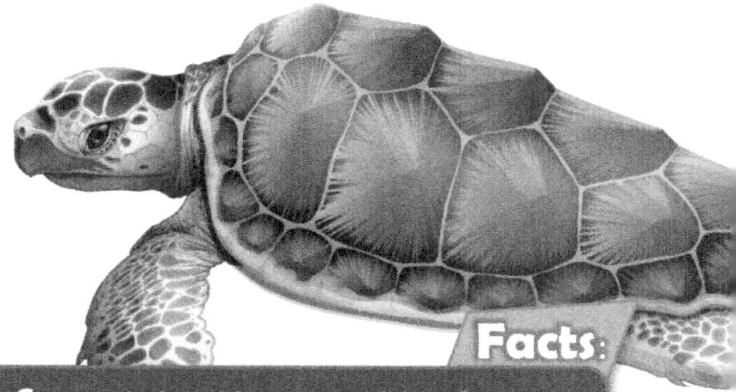

(1) A sea turtle crawls onto a beach at 11:28 PM. She digs a nest, laying her eggs, buries them, and returns to the water by 1:44 AM. How long was this turtle on land?

(2) Sea turtles can make many nests and lay several clutches of eggs in one season. If a turtle lays 90 eggs in each clutch, how many eggs will it lay in 3 clutches?

**Facts:**

- **Sea turtle hatchlings have lots of predators, but adult sea turtles have few.**
- **Humans pose the most risk to sea turtles.**
- **Pollution can harm turtles, and human activity on beaches can disrupt nesting.**

(3) Most turtle hatchlings will not survive very long. Out of 110 hatchlings, 14 are eaten by racoons, 8 are eaten by crabs, and 25 are eaten by seagulls before they make it to the ocean. How many of the hatchlings do make it to the ocean?

(4) Some people estimate that only 1 hatching out of a 1,000 will live to adulthood. If this is true, how many hatchlings would be expected to live out of 9,000 hatchlings?

**Facts:**

- **Sea turtles swim thousands of miles while migrating and can dive thousands of feet below the ocean's surface.**
- **They can't hide in their shells. Their shells and flippers are suited for swimming, not hiding.**

(5) The leatherback is the largest sea turtle species. One can weigh over 2,000 pounds. How many 200-pound men are needed to equal the weight of such a large leatherback?

(6) Researchers attached transmitters to the shells of turtles, so satellites could track where the turtle traveled in the ocean. If the researchers placed transmitters on 16 turtles the first night, 19 turtle the second night, and 13 turtles the third night, how many transmitters did they place?

**Trivia:**

- **What predators do adult sea turtles have?**

Name: ____________________

Score:

① Mike and Peter competed in a car race and need to refill their vehicles. Fuel at the racetrack costs £1.32 per liter. How much would it cost Peter to pay for both of their fuel if they need to purchase 10 liters of track fuel each?

② The racetrack reported that 1,842 adult tickets and 607 children's tickets were sold. How many tickets is that all together?

③ There are a total of 25 racecars signed up for the event. If 4 of them were disqualified and 2 didn't show up, how many racecars were able to compete?

④ Mike's racecar travels at an average speed of 118 miles per hour. How many miles will he likely travel if he continuously races for an hour and a half?

⑤ Each lap around the racetrack is 2 miles, and the racecars need to complete 100 laps. Peter has already completed 57 laps. How many more miles will he need to travel to finish the race?

⑥ Peter finished in 1st place, and Mike finished in 6th place. If the cash prize for the winner is £15,000 and then the amount of the cash prize decreases by £2,000 for each subsequent car that finishes the race, what was the size of Mike's cash prize?

Name: ____________________

Score:

**Facts:**

- **A newborn's brain has about 100 billion neurons. An adult's brain has roughly the same amount.**
- **You may not gain neurons as you age but you do grow trillions of synapses to connect your neurons.**
- **Our brains don't fully develop until about age 25.**

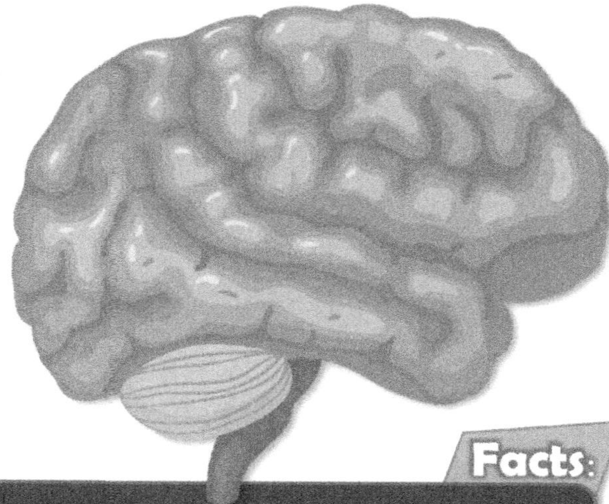

(1) A baby's brain will grow about 3 times its size during its first year of life. If a newborn's brain weighs 375 grams, how much will its brain weigh on its 1st birthday?

(2) If one neuron has 2,531 synapses connected to it when a baby is born and the same neuron has 14,000 synapses connected to it 2 years later, how many more synapses did the neuron grow?

**Facts:**

- **Neurons create small electrical signals to communicate with the rest of the body.**
- **These signals travel about 250 miles per hour.**
- **The average brain makes about 20 watts of energy—enough to light a small light bulb.**

(3) A person could easily have one hundred fifteen trillion, eight hundred four billion, three hundred sixty-six million, fifty-seven thousand, two hundred ninety-five brain synapses. What is that number written in standard form?

(4) Brains need more oxygen when they're working on complex problems. If your brain uses 20% of your oxygen when resting but 37% when working on a difficult math problem, how much more oxygen is it using while solving the problem?

**Facts:**

- **Approximately 60% of your brain is fat.**
- **Most of this fat is omega-3 fatty acids.**
- **Omega-3 fatty acids are essential for brain function, learning, and memory.**

(5) If someone eats 2,000 calories in a day, their brain will likely use one fifth of those calories. How many of the calories is that?

(6) If a person usually eats 300 milligrams of Omega-3 a day but today eats only 163 milligrams, how much less Omega-3 did they eat today?

**Trivia:**

- **What foods contain omega-3 fatty acids?**

Name: ____________________

Score:

① Dr. Sanchez is a paleontologist. She is currently overseeing 3 separate dig sites. So far, her crew has removed 319 buckets of dirt from the first dig site, 132 buckets of dirt from the second dig site, and 185 buckets of dirt from the third dig site. How many buckets of dirt is that all together?

② The digging started on Monday. By Thursday they had unearthed a total of 192 dinosaur bones. On average, how many dinosaur bones is that per day?

③ The longest bone found was 62 cm long. The shortest bone was 6 cm long. How much longer was the longest bone than the shortest bone?

④ Clair and Greg cleaned bones for 9 hours today. If they each cleaned 3 bones an hour, how many bones did they clean today?

⑤ If 105 of the bones have been found at the first dig site and 58 of the bones have been found at the second dig site, how many of the 192 bones were found at the third dig site?

⑥ The youngest set of bones is estimated to be 65.8 million years old. The oldest set of bones is estimated to be 142 million years old. If these estimates are correct, how much older is the oldest set of bones than the youngest set of bones?

Name: ____________________

Score:

**Facts:**

- **All magnets have a north pole and south pole.**
- **If a magnet is cut in half there will be two magnets, and each will have its own north and south pole.**

(1) If you have 8 magnets and cut them all in half, then cut all the halves in half, how many magnets would you have?

(2) If 1 magnet has 2 poles (a north and south pole), how many poles would 6 magnets have?

**Facts:**

- **Earth is a gigantic magnet. It also has a north and south pole.**
- **A compass needle follows the pull of Earth's magnetic field.**

(3) Junk yards often use cranes with giant electromagnets to lift iron scraps. If one crane can lift 12 tons of iron and a second crane can lift 25 tons of iron, how much more can the second crane lift?

(4) If a regular passenger train (the kind with wheels on a train track) travels 125 miles per hour and a maglev train travels 300 miles per hour, how much faster is the maglev train?

**Facts:**

- **Maglev trains use magnetic levitation to float on air and travel incredibly fast.**
- **Do you know someone who had an MRI scan? Magnetic resonance imaging (MRI) can make pictures of your inner body organs.**

(5) If a maglev train is traveling 300 miles per hour, how many hours would it take the train to travel 1,200 miles?

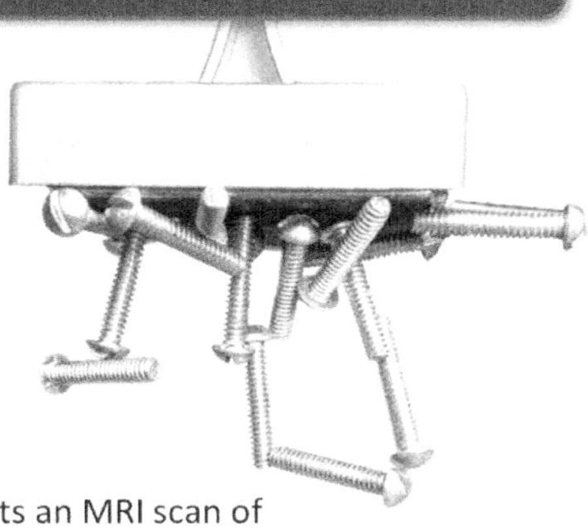

(6) Molly fell off her bike and was not wearing a helmet. A doctor wants an MRI scan of Molly's brain to see if it was damaged. Molly was placed in the MRI machine at 3:46 pm and the scan did not finish until 4:12 pm.  How long did Molly's MRI scan take?

**Trivia:**

- **What is a cow magnet?**

Name: ____________________

Score:

1. If a news channel delivers an average of 32 news reports on weekdays and an average of 45 news reports each day of the weekend, how many news reports does it deliver in the average week?

2. This news channel has a total of 54 reporters. If 27 of the reporters are women, how many reporters are men?

3. Of the 54 reporters, 13 of them are hired full-time. The rest are part-time reporters. If full-time reporters are paid £1,200 a week and part-time reporters are paid £600 a week, how much does the news channel spend each week to pay its reporters?

4. Lea is one of the reporters. She delivered 12 local news reports, 5 sports reports, 8 world news reports, and 3 entertainment news reports last year. How many reports was that all together?

5. Megan usually only delivers reports that are 4 minutes long. But today, she needs to deliver a 20-minute special report about a local fire. How many times longer is this special report than the length of her usual report?

6. It is a weekend, and 45 news reports need to be reported today. If the news channel wants to deliver all these reports within the next 9 hours, on average, how many reports will it need to broadcast each hour?

# Day 18

Name: ____________________

Score:

**Facts:**

- **House flies can taste things with their feet.**
- **They also have sticky pads on their feet that allow them to walk on walls and ceilings.**

(1) If each female house fly can lay 500 eggs in its lifetime, how many eggs could 6 females lay?

(2) An egg usually hatches within 24 hours after it's laid. If an egg was laid 6 hours ago, what's the longest amount of time it will probably take before it hatches?

**Facts:**

- **House flies only live about 15 to 30 days.**
- **Females can lay 500 eggs during that time.**
- **House flies can only drink food because their mouths can't eat solid objects.**
- **Liquid food passes through their digestive system quickly, which is why house flies poop almost every time they land.** (Remember that next time one lands on your arm.)

(3) A larva hatched from an egg and lived 7 days in that stage, eating lots of food before making a pupa (which is kind of like a cocoon). If it spends 20 days as a pupa before emerging as a house fly, how long did it take to go from the egg stage to fly stage?

(4) A house fly lays 500 eggs, but only 83 of them survive to become house flies. How many did not survive?

(5) If a house fly beats its wings 200 times a second, how many seconds would it take for it to beat its wings 10,000 times?

(6) Oliver accidentally left fruit out while on vacation. When he returned, there were 36 flies in his house. Over the next day, he was able to swat 28 of them, but then 9 more hatched. How many flies are in his home now?

**Trivia:**

- **If house flies don't eat solid food, why do they always want to land on the solid foods we eat?**

Name: ____________________

Score:

① A post office has 48 employees. 6 of the employees are service clerks, 25 are mail carriers, and the rest are mail sorters. How many mail sorters are there?

② If the post office processes an average of 180,000 pieces of mail a day, how many pieces of mail would it process every 30 days?

③ There are 25 mail carriers and together they deliver about 180,000 pieces of mail a day. On average, how many pieces of mail is that for each mail carrier?

④ Eric, a mail carrier, had 18 full bags of mail to deliver today. He already delivered the mail from 6 of the bags. If each bag contains 400 pieces of mail, how many more pieces of mail does he still need to deliver today?

⑤ The post office had 15,000 envelopes, but customers purchased 5,704 of the envelopes last week and 6,142 of the envelopes this week. How many envelopes does the post office have left?

⑥ A customer wants a box to be delivered. Emma, the mail clerk, explains that it will cost £9.45 to deliver the box. If the customer gives Emma a 20-pound note to pay for the delivery, how much change should Emma give the customer back?

# Day 20

Name: ______________________

Score:

**Facts:**

- **Moisture in a popcorn kernel expands when heated, but the shell prevents it from expanding very much.**
- **Pressure builds inside the kernel until the shell cracks.**
- **The insides push out as moisture expands to steam.**

① If 1 liter of kernels makes 32 liters of popcorn, how many liters of popcorn would 4 liters of kernels make?

② A popcorn kernel was 22 °C before someone heated it. If it popped when it was 180 °C, how many degrees did it have to increase before popping?

**Facts:**

- **Native Americans were making popcorn over 7,000 years ago.**
- **A couple hundred years ago, people ate popcorn for breakfast, adding milk and sprinkles of sugar to it.**
- **Modern health diets are making breakfast popcorn popular again.**

③ If it costs a theater 43 cents to make a bag of popcorn and it sells each popcorn bag for 6 pounds, how much of a profit does the theater make from a bag of popcorn?

caramel covered popcorn

④ If a theater sells 16,000 bags of popcorn each month, how many bags of popcorn would it sell in a year?

**Facts:**

- **Popcorn is a healthy food that has a lot of fiber, protein, vitamins, and minerals.**
- **It's the excessive toppings such as salt, butter, and sugar that can be unhealthy.**

⑤ If 100 grams of popped popcorn contains 9 grams of protein, how many grams of popcorn would you have to eat to consume 27 grams of protein?

⑥ The United States is the largest producer and consumer of popcorn, and Nebraska grows more popcorn kernels than any other state. If Nebraska produced 296 million pounds of kernels last year and 311 million pounds of kernels this year, how much more did it produce this year?

**Trivia:**

- **There are two different kinds of popcorn—mushroom shaped popcorn and butterfly shaped popcorn. But most theaters only sell butterfly popcorn. Do you know why?**

Name: ____________________

Score:

1. If a city experiences an average of 42 thunderstorms a year, how many will the city likely experience every 5 years?

2. A large thunderstorm can produce ten times the amount of rainfall an average thunderstorm can. If an average thunderstorm produces 2,000 metric tons of rainfall, how much does a large thunderstorm produce?

3. A large thunderstorm passed over the city of Dublin. 4 hours later that thunderstorm had reached Manchester. If Dublin and Manchester are about 160 miles away from each other, what was the thunderstorm's average speed per hour?

4. Strong winds and lightning caused a power outage in a city near Manchester. 15,042 homes lost power, but a few minutes later, power returned to 7,461 of the homes. The rest still do not have power. How many of the homes still don't have power?

5. A thunderstorm damaged 28 houses in Manchester, 17 houses in Stretford, and 6 in Stockport. What is the total number of houses that were damaged by the thunderstorm?

6. The city purchased new electrical poles to replace ones that had been damaged by the storm. If 20 electrical poles cost the city £9,000, what was the cost per pole?

REAL LIFE NUMBERS

# Day 22

Name: ____________________

Score:

**Facts:**

- **Toothpastes are abrasives that help to grind plaque and food from your teeth when they are brushed.**
- **People have made toothpastes for over 7,000 years, often adding eggshells or pumice stones as abrasives.**

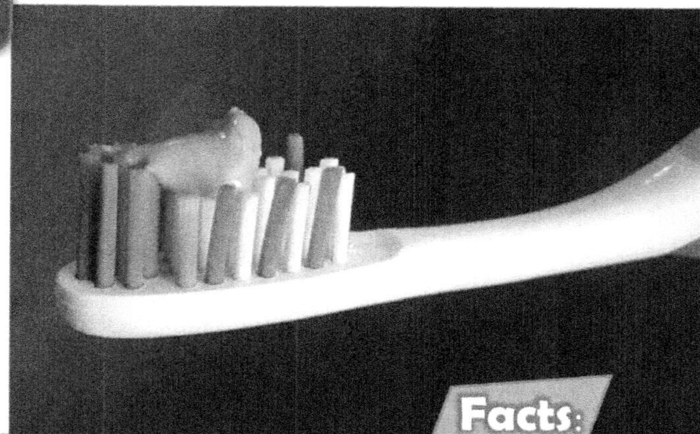

1. Many dentists recommend brushing your teeth for 2 minutes, twice a day. How many seconds is that a day?

2. If an old toothpaste recipe called for 3 crushed eggshells, how many eggshells would be needed if a person wanted to make 3 batches of the recipe?

**Facts:**

- **Fluoride toothpastes may offer additional cavity protection because low concentrations of fluoride help strengthen and remineralize tooth enamel.**
- **Large amounts of fluoride are harmful (poisonous), so don't swallow fluoride toothpaste. Speak with a dentist before changing your oral health routines.**

3. If a tooth had 2,384,015 bacteria on it before it was brushed and 93,643 bacteria on it after it was brushed, how much bacteria was brushed away?

4. Molly's dentist recommended that her little brother not use fluoride toothpaste until he is 48 months old, because she was afraid he would swallow the toothpaste before then. How many years old is that?
*(Repeated addition may help.)*

**Facts:**

- **Many dentists say that you only need to use a pea-size blob of toothpaste when brushing.**
- **Advertisements from toothpaste companies are likely the reason so many people put a ribbon of toothpaste onto their toothbrush.**

5. If a pea-sized blob of toothpaste weighs 0.25 grams and Molly uses 0.8 grams of toothpaste when brushing her teeth, how much more toothpaste is she using than a pea-sized blob?

6. If Molly is able to use one tube of toothpaste for 57 days before it runs out, how many days would Molly be able to use 4 tubes of toothpaste?

**Trivia:**

- **For centuries, urine was a common ingredient found in toothpaste recipes. Why is that?**

Name: ____________________

Score:

(1) Luis drives to work 5 days a week and gets stuck in a traffic jam for an average of 21 minutes each morning. How much time does he spend in the traffic jams each week?

(2) Luis is currently in a traffic jam on the highway. He's only able to drive 30 meters every 5 minutes. His turn off the highway is still 120 meters away. At his current speed, how long will it take him to reach the turn?

(3) It took Luis 1 hour and 4 minutes to get to work yesterday, so he decided to take a new route today. The new route allowed him to get to work in 48 minutes. How much faster was the new route?

(4) The city determined that many of the traffic jams were being caused by people violating traffic laws. The mayor asked the city police to better enforce these laws. The next day, officers ticketed 7 drivers for disregarding traffic lights, 12 drivers for failing to signal before changing lanes, and 23 drivers for speeding. How many traffic violation tickets is that?

(5) Each driver needs to pay a fine for every violation they commit. The fine for disregarding traffic lights is £145, the fine for failing to signal is £100, and the fine for speeding is £120. Using the information in question 4, how many pounds' worth of fines did the officers issue that day?

(6) Mike was caught disregarding a traffic light and failing to signal before changing lanes. An officer wrote him a ticket for each of these violations. How much money will Mike need to pay?

Name: ____________________

Score:

**Facts:**

- **A child's heart usually beats faster than an adult's.**
- **A person's heart is about the size of their fist.**

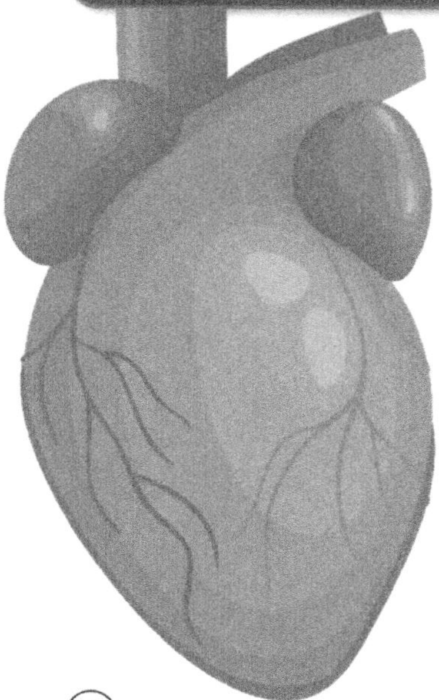

1. If a newborn baby's heart is beating 115 times a minute and an adult's heart is beating 80 beats a minute, how many more times will the newborn's heart beat during a 5 minute period?

2. If your heart beats about 4,800 times an hour, how many times will it beat in 3 hours?

**Facts:**

- **The beating sound of your heart is caused by the opening and closing of your heart valves.**
- **People have 4 heart valves that help to stop blood from flowing in the wrong direction.**
- **A heart murmur can occur when a heart valve is not working properly. Blood does not flow normally and creates a murmuring noise as it passes through the valve.**

3. Mia's heart rate was 76 beats per minute before she ran a race, and it was 159 beats per minute right after she finished the race. How much faster was her heart beating after the race?

4. Zack also took his heart rate before and after the race. His heart rate was 82 beats per minute before the race. After the race, it had increased by 67 beats per minute. But when he took it again two minutes after the race, his heart rate had already slowed by 28 beats per minute. How fast was Zach's heart beating two minutes after the race?

5. If the heart pumps out 60 mL of blood each time it beats, how many heart beats would it take it to pump out 900 mL of blood?

6. Bethany's grandfather needed open heart surgery. The surgery started at 10:53 in the morning and ended 4 hours and 32 minutes later. What time did the surgery end?

**Trivia:**

- **How many times can a person's heart beat in their lifetime?**

Name: ____________________

Score:

1. Bill's bakery sells an average of 800 cookies a day and 450 cupcakes a day. How many more cookies is that each week?

2. Bill baked 320 cookies in the morning, 250 cookies in the afternoon, and 270 cookies in the evening. How many cookies did he bake that day?

3. A bread slicer can slice 3 loaves of bread a minute. At this rate, how long would it take to slice 540 loaves of bread?

4. A school needs 91 sandwiches for a school picnic. The school cook purchased 8 loaves of bread to make the sandwiches. If each loaf contains 24 slices of bread and each sandwich requires 2 slices of bread, how many slices will be left over after the sandwiches are prepared?

5. The bakery only has 2 bags of flour left. Bill plans to use this flour to make as many cupcakes as possible. The cupcake recipe calls for 20 cups of flour and makes 100 cupcakes. If each bag contains 120 cups of flour, how many cupcakes can Bill make?

6. Bill's bakery made £12,500 last month. He used some of this money to buy £5,210 worth of new ingredients. He also spent £450 to fix a broken oven. How much money did Bill's bakery have left after these two expenses?

Name: ____________________

Score:

**Facts:**

- **Squid are invertebrates (they have no backbones).**
- **They are closely related to clams and snails.**
- **There are hundreds of different squid species.**

**Facts:**

- **The colossal squid is probably the world's biggest invertebrate.**
- **We know little about colossal squid or how big they can get.**
- **Some are over 45 feet long and weigh 1,100 pounds.**

1. If a giant squid weighs 600 pounds and a colossal squid weighs 1,100 pounds, how much heavier is the colossal squid?

2. If a school bus is 10 feet shorter than a 45-foot long colossal squid, how long is the school bus?

3. Squid are skilled predators that like to eat things like fish, clams, and crabs. If one squid ate 54 fish, 13 clams, and 9 crabs this week, how many times more fish did it eat than crabs?

4. If a research crew wants to film a giant squid, they will need to lower their camera 2,000 feet below the ocean surface. If their camera lowers 50 feet every minute and it is already 800 feet down, how much longer will it take their camera to reach a depth of 2,000 feet?

**Facts:**

- **Squid can change colors to blend with their surroundings.**
- **They can release ink into the water like octopuses do to escape from predators.**
- **People eat lots of squid. It's often called calamari, which is the Italian word for squid.**

5. Sperm whales love to eat squid. If 3 sperm whales eat a total of 144 squid in a day, how many squid is that per whale?

6. Squid can regenerate their arms if one is eaten by a predator. If 2 feet of a squid's arm is eaten and it grows 9 inches back the first year and 8 inches back the second year, how many more inches does the arm have to grow to be back to normal size?

**Trivia:**

- **What is the length of the smallest squid species?**

Name: ____________________

Score:

① A hospital has a total of 12 floors. Each floor has 35 rooms, and each room has 2 beds. How many beds does the hospital have?

② Each room in the hospital can accommodate 2 patients. How many rooms are needed if 38 new patients need to be admitted to the hospital?

③ There are 198 medical staff members currently working in the hospital. 34 are doctors, 95 are nurses, and the rest are assistants. How many assistants are there?

④ A cardiologist usually spends 20 minutes consulting with each patient. At this rate, how many patients could the cardiologist consult within 6 hours?

⑤ A medical pump is currently giving Bethany 70 mL of medicine each hour. At this rate, how long will it take the pump to give Bethany a total of 350 mL?

⑥ The hospital staff uses about 23,000 gloves throughout the day. How many boxes of gloves is that if each box contains 200 gloves?

Name: ____________________

Score:

**Facts:**

- **Cinnamon is one of mankind's oldest known spices.**
- **In ancient Egypt, it was worth more than gold.**

(1) If one gram of cinnamon used to be worth 15 grams of silver, how many grams of silver would 5 grams of cinnamon have been worth?

(2) The cinnamon trees can grow to be 15 meters tall. If a tree is 9 meters tall now, how much taller will it have to grow to become 15 meters tall?

**Facts:**

- **Cinnamon comes from a cinnamon tree.**
- **The outer bark of the tree is peeled away, so that the inner bark can be collected.**
- **The inner bark is the cinnamon. It takes about a week for this inner bark to dry.**
- **The inner bark curls and darkens as it dries, creating cinnamon sticks.**
- **Cinnamon sticks can be ground into cinnamon powder.**

(3) Cinnamon was harvested and started to dry 4 days ago. If it takes 7 days for it to fully dry, how many more days of drying are left?

(4) If the farm produced 24,431 sticks of cinnamon last year and 26,072 sticks this year, how many more sticks did it produce this year?

**Facts:**

- **Moderate amounts of cinnamon have many good health benefits.**
- **It can be good for your heart and brain.**
- **It's been used in medicines for centuries.**

(5) If it takes 260 of the farm's cinnamon sticks to make 1 kg of cinnamon, how many of their sticks would it take to make 6 kg of cinnamon?

(6) Theo wants to make 50 cookies for his birthday party. If it takes 12 grams of cinnamon powder to make 100 cookies, how many grams of cinnamon will he need to make 50 cookies?

**Trivia:**

- **Where is cinnamon grown?**

# Day 29

Name: ____________________

Score:

(1) Jacob's farm has 3,280 chickens and 4 chicken barns to keep them in. How many chickens is that per barn?

(2) If each of Jacob's chickens can lay 250 eggs a year, how many eggs could 3,280 chickens lay a year?

(3) Jacob decided to sell 545 of his chickens. If he had 3,280 chickens before this sale, how many chickens does he have now?

(4) Jacob spent £800 buying more sacks of chicken feed. If each sack of feed costs £32, how many sacks of feed did Jacob get?

(5) The chickens in each of the 4 barns eat 20 pounds of feed a day. If each sack of feed weighs 60 pounds, how many days would it take the chickens on Jacob's farm to eat 12 sacks of feed?

(6) Jacob wants to build 3 more chicken barns. If each barn will cost £37,400 to build, how much will it cost to build all 3 barns?

# Day 30

Name: ____________________

Score:

**Facts:**

- **Llamas and alpacas are closely related species.**
- **Both are from South America.**

① Llamas are a little taller than alpacas. A llama's average height is perhaps 168 cm tall. Alpaca average about 137 cm tall. How many cm taller is the average llama than alpaca?

**Facts:**

- **Llamas and alpacas have been domesticated for 6,000 years.**
- **They provide meat and fleece. Llamas are also pack animals.**
- **Alpaca fleece is very soft and used to be reserved for royalty.**
- **Their fleece is water resistant and warmer than sheep wool.**

② Llamas are also heavier. A llama often weighs 110 kg while alpacas typically weight 65 kg. How much heavier are llamas?

③ Llamas are often used as pack animals. If a llama can carry 36 kg of weight, how many 12-kg packs could it carry for you?

④ If an alpaca produces about 4 kg of fur a year and the owner can sell every half kg of fur for £50, how much money would the owner get for this fur?

⑤ If an alpaca farmer has a herd of 8 alpacas and each produces 4 kg of fur, how many kg of fur would the whole herd produce?

⑥ The alpaca fur was used to make 1 blanket, 4 hats, and 2 shirts. If the blanket sells for £250, each hat sells for £45, and the shirts sell for £70 each, how much were these items worth all together?

**Trivia:**

- **Why is alpaca fur so warm?**

Name: ____________________

Score:

① A tanker ship is being loaded with oil. It can hold 2 million barrels of oil, but currently only has 168,324 barrels of oil on board. How many more barrels of oil need to be loaded before the tanker ship is full?

② If one barrel of oil currently costs £92, how much would 2 million barrels of oil be worth?

③ Melisa is the oil tanker's captain. If she is paid £6,500 a month to captain the ship, how much money will she be paid to captain the ship for a year?

④ The Suez Canal is nearly 195 km long. How fast was Melisa's ship traveling if it takes her 15 hours to pass through the canal?

⑤ While in the open ocean, Melisa's ship can travel 30 km per hour. At this rate, it will take her ship 10 days to travel from the Suez Canal to the Port of London. How many kilometers will Melisa's ship be traveling for this journey?

⑥ Melisa expects it to take 25 hours to unload the 2 million barrels of oil. At this rate, how many barrels of oil can be unloaded each hour?

Name: ____________________

Score:

**Facts:**

- **Native Americans in Central and South America were cultivating pineapples over a thousand years ago.**
- **When Europeans encountered this fruit, they thought it resembled a pinecone, so they called it a pineapple.**

1. If one pineapple contains 116 berries and a larger pineapple contains 143 berries, how many more berries does the larger pineapple have?

2. If one wild pineapple has 2,368 seeds and another wild pineapple has 2,055 seeds, how may seeds do they have together?

3. If 1,800 of the seeds were planted, but 453 of these seeds didn't grow, how many did grow?

**Facts:**

- **A pineapple is a bunch of berries that have fused into one fruit. (Can you see the round outlines of the berries in the picture below?)**
- **Wild pineapples have seeds but cultivated pineapples are bred not to have seeds.**
- **If the top leafy part is cut off and put in dirt, it can grow into a pineapple plant.**
- **A pineapple plant can grow to be 6 feet wide and 6 feet tall.**

4. After a pineapple top was planted, it took 14 months for it to grow flowers. After that, it took 11 more months to grow some fruit. Altogether, how many months did it take this pineapple top to grow some fruit?

5. If a pineapple plantation grows 28,000 pineapple plants per acre, how many plants would a 3-acre plantation have?

6. Mark bought 7 pineapples from a plantation. If each pineapple weighs 2 pounds, how much do the 7 pineapples weigh all together?

**Trivia:**

- **What country grows the most pineapples?**

Name: ____________________

Score:

(1) William became a plumber when he was 23 years old.
If he has been working for 25 years now, what is his present age?

(2) William charges his customers £55 for every hour he works.
If he spent 2 hours removing a broken pipe and 3 hours installing a new pipe, how much money should he charge?

(3) William explained to Anna that she will need a total of 27 feet of new pipes installed in her house, 15 feet for her kitchen and the rest for her bathroom. How many feet of pipes does Anna's bathroom need?

(4) If each foot of pipe costs £5, how much will Anna need to spend to purchase all 27 feet of pipes?

(5) William can install 6 feet of pipes each hour. At this rate, how long would it take him to install all 27 feet of pipes?

(6) William tells Anna that it would be a good idea to let him fix her leaky faucet too.
He estimates that the faucet is leaking 3 gallons of water a day.
How many gallons of water is that a year?

**Facts:**

- **A meteor is a space rock that enters Earth's atmosphere.**
- **If a meteor hits the Earth, it's called a meteorite.**

Name: ____________________

Score:

1. Rifle bullets can travel at speeds of about 3,000 km per hour. If a meteor enters Earth's atmosphere at 48,000 km an hour, how many times faster is it traveling than the speed of a bullet?

2. Lava is often 1,100 °C. If a meteor heats up to 1,500 °C when it enters the atmosphere, how much hotter is it than lava?

**Facts:**

- **Meteors are often called shooting stars because they can produce bright light when they burn.**
- **Meteors burn because they enter the atmosphere at very fast speeds, creating friction and heat.**
- **Most meteors are about the size of a grain of sand and completely burn before hitting the ground.**

3. Many scientists believe a meteorite impact helped to cause the extinction of the dinosaurs. This meteor was probably at least 9 km wide and made a crater about 175 km wide. How much wider was the crater than the meteorite?

**Facts:**

- **Comets are large chunks of dirty space ice.**
- **If a comet passes too close to the sun it melts and leaves a trail of dust and space rocks.**
- **When Earth passes through a comet trail the dust and pebbles create a meteor shower.**
- **Extreme meteor showers are called meteor storms and have over 1,000 meteors an hour.**

4. The Leonid meteor shower becomes a meteor storm every 33 years. The 1999 Leonid meteor storm often produced a meteor every 2 seconds. How many meteors is that per minute?

5. In 1833, the Leonid meteor storm was so intense many people thought the world was ending. Some people estimate that there were 40 meteors every second. At this rate, how many meteors would have been seen in 15 seconds?

6. There are different types of meteorites. Some are very rare to find and are more valuable than gold, platinum, or diamonds. If one meteorite sold for £73,200 and a second sold for £259,000, how much were these two meteorites worth together?

**Trivia:**

- **How do people find meteorites?**

Name: ____________________

Score:

(1) Jackson and his brother Noah purchased a new videogame. The videogame normally costs £45, but they bought it on sale for £38. How much money did the sale save them?

(2) If Jackson and Noah split the cost of the £38 evenly, how much money did they each have to pay?

(3) During the first game, Noah got 356 points in the first round, 485 points in the second round, and 375 points in the 3rd round. What was the total number of points Noah got in the game?

(4) During the fourth game, Jackson's score was 3 times as much as Noah's score. If Noah had scored 265 points, how many points did Jackson score?

(5) Jackson eventually received a score of 3,205 points. This beat their previous record by 438 points. What was their previous record?

(6) It took the brothers 6 hours to finish playing 9 games. On average, how long did it take to finish each game?

Name: ____________________

Score:

**Facts:**

- **Earthquakes can cause huge waves called <u>tsunamis</u>.**
- **Tsunamis can be over 100 feet tall and often cause more death and destruction than the initial earthquake.**

(1) Most tsunamis are not tall when they begin. As they enter shallow water, their speed slows, and they grow much taller. A tsunami in the open ocean that is only 2 feet tall could easily grow to be 64 feet high by the time it hits shore. How many times taller would such a wave have grown?

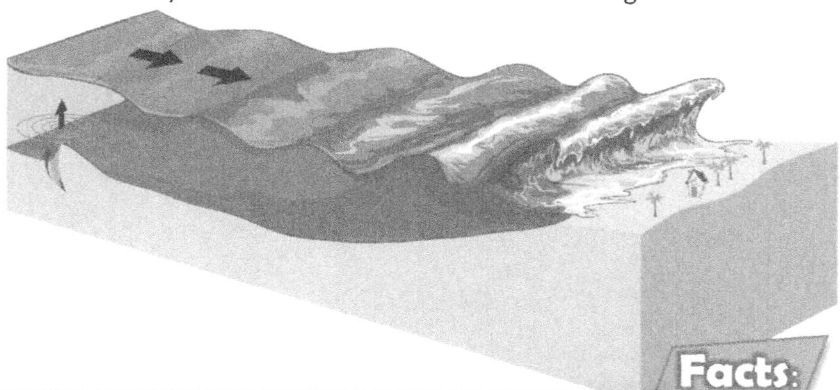

(2) A tsunami in the deep ocean can travel at speeds of over 600 mph. At this rate, how long would it take a tsunami in the deep ocean to travel 3,000 miles?

**Facts:**

| | Wind Wave | Tsunami (Deep Ocean) | Tsunami (Shallow Water) |
|---|---|---|---|
| Wave Speed | 20 mph | 600 mph | 30 mph |
| Wavelength | 300 feet | 300,000 feet | Less than 10,000 feet |
| Wave Period | 20 seconds | 2 hours or less | 2 hours or less |
| Wave Height | 8 feet | 3 feet | 100 feet |
| Wave Example | | | |

Critical Thinking: Why does the wave example for the deep ocean tsunami look flat?

(3) A tsunami traveling through the deep ocean at 600 mph will often slow to 30 mph by the time it reaches shore. How many times slower is that?

(4) One Tsunami wave entered a harbor at 9:43 AM. The next wave entered the harbor at 11:06 AM. What was the period between the two waves?

(5) A wind wave is a wave caused by the power of wind. Using the examples in the chart above, how many times longer is the wavelength of a deep ocean tsunami than a wind wave?

(6) On average, Hawaii experiences a severe tsunami every 7 years. If this average continues, how many severe tsunamis would you expect Hawaii to experience over the next 35 years?

**Trivia:**

- **How do people protect themselves from tsunamis?**

24 9 0 + 5 7 1 3 − 6 8

# Day 37

Name: ____________________

Score:

1. Mr. Crab opened a restaurant. 389 guests ate there on the opening day, 412 guests yesterday, and 476 guests today. In a span of these first three days, how many guests did the restaurant serve?

2. The restaurant has 25 tables. Each table has 8 chairs. What is the total seating capacity of the restaurant if all chairs are occupied?

3. Mr. Crab hired 45 employees for his restaurant. It consists of 2 managers, 7 cashiers, 15 cooks and the rest servers. How many servers are there in the restaurant?

4. Patrick and his friends ordered 3 steak platters and paid £57 for them. How much does one steak platter cost?

5. Sandy's family went to Mr. Crab's restaurant. She bought 2 seafood platters for £26.25 each, a beef platter for £17.78, and 3 pork platters for £16.59 each. Sandy paid for these meals with a £50 restaurant gift card and the rest she paid in cash. How much cash did she use?

6. Mr. Crab's restaurant has 6 full racks of large plates and 5 full racks of small plates. If each rack holds 24 plates, how many plates are on the racks?

Name: ______________________

Score:

**Facts:**

- **Salt normally comes from either evaporating seawater or mining rock salt from the ground.**
- **Rock salt is usually the salt deposits left behind after ancient salt lakes or seabeds dried up.**

(1) Sea salt companies evaporate seawater and sell the salt that's left behind. If a company made 3,540 kg of salt yesterday and 3,750 kg today, how many more kg did they make today?

(2) If one liter of seawater has about 35 grams of salt in it, how much salt would you expect to get if you evaporated 20 liters of seawater?

(3) If one salt mine produces 1,850 kg of salt a day and another mine produces 1,460 kg a day, how many kg would they both produce in a week?

**Facts:**

- **Roman soldiers were sometimes paid with salt, which is how the word "salary" was invented. "Sal" means salt in Latin.**
- **The saying "not worth his salt" was used when a soldier didn't do a good job.**

**Facts:**

- **If used properly, salt makes food taste better and protects it from spoiling.**
- **You need salt to live, but too much or too little is not healthy for you.**
- **Salt reduces the melting point of ice, so it's often spread on icy roads.**

(4) If 8 Roman soldiers were given 48 grams of salt to share evenly, how many grams would each get?

(5) The melting point of ice is 0 °C. Luna sprinkled salt on her icy sidewalk, and this lowered the melting point to -14 °C. How many degrees lower is that?

(6) If the city of Winnipeg decided to buy 20,000 tons of road salt before this winter started and ended up using 17,352 tons, how many tons of salt does the city have left over?

**Trivia:**

- **How much salt should a person eat?**

Name: ____________________

Score:

① A concert is being planned. If all 5,000 tickets to the concert are sold for £70 a ticket, and half the money from the ticket sales are donated to a cancer research foundation, how much money would be donated?

② Two days before the concert, there were only 3,358 tickets sold. How many more still needed to be sold to sell all 5,000 tickets?

③ The ticketing team paid a radio station to help advertise the concert. If the team had to pay a total of £700 for a commercial advertising the concert to be aired 20 times, what was the cost of each airing?

④ There will be a total of 9 bands performing at the concert. If each band performs for 25 minutes, how long will the concert last?

⑤ T-shirts are sold at the concert. They normally cost £25 each, but there is a special offer to buy 4 t-shirts for £80. If someone purchases 4 t-shirts, how much would they be paying for each shirt?

⑥ At the concert, Jam bought a glow-stick for himself and a glowing stick for each of his seven friends. If each glowing stick costs £7, what was the total cost of the glow sticks?

Name: ____________________

Score:

**Facts:**

- **Clouds form when invisible water vapor condenses into visible water droplets or ice crystals.**

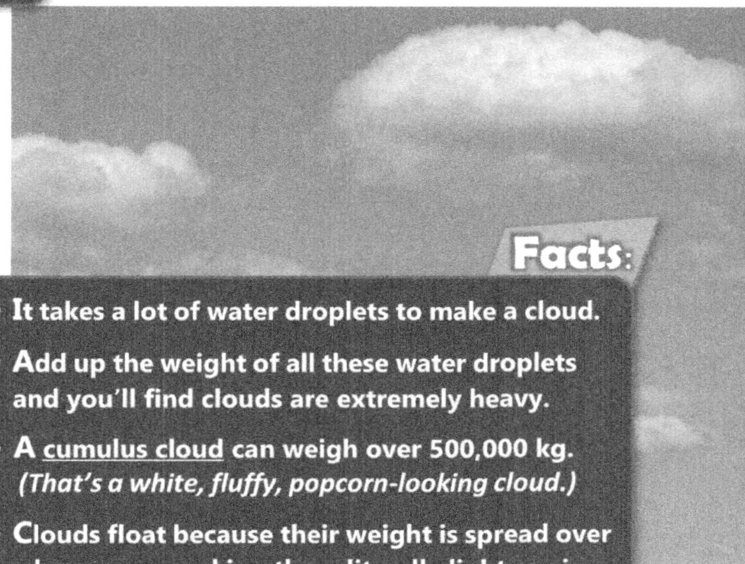

① If a cumulus cloud weighed 165,000 kg in the morning but grew to 500,000 kg by the afternoon, how much more weight did the cloud gain?

**Facts:**

- **It takes a lot of water droplets to make a cloud.**
- **Add up the weight of all these water droplets and you'll find clouds are extremely heavy.**
- **A cumulus cloud can weigh over 500,000 kg.** ***(That's a white, fluffy, popcorn-looking cloud.)***
- **Clouds float because their weight is spread over a large area, making them literally light as air.**

② If one cloud weighs 382,000 kg, a second cloud weighs 416,000 kg, and a third weighs 309,000 kg, how much do these three clouds weigh all together?

③ If a cloud weighs 420,000 kg and a blue whale weighs 140,000 kg, how many blue whales are needed to equal the weight of this cloud?
*(Repeated addition may help find the answer.)*

④ If the flat bottom of a cumulus cloud is 1,900 meters above ground and the top of the cloud is 3,200 meters above ground, how tall is the cumulus cloud?

⑤ A 1,200-meter-tall cumulus cloud grew into a 13,200-meter-tall thunderstorm cloud, called a cumulonimbus. How many times larger did the cloud grow?

**Facts:**

- **Contrails are the condensation trails that jets make when they fly at high altitudes.**
- **Warm moist air from jet engines cool and condense, forming long man-made clouds.**

⑥ The air where contrails form is often much colder than air near the ground. For example, a jet 10,000 meters above the ground could be passing through air that is -54 °C, while the ground temperature below it is 26 °C. In this example, how much colder is the air by the jet than the air by the ground?

**Trivia:**

- **What is a cloud called when it's at ground level?**

Name: ____________________

Score:

① A rare diamond mysteriously disappeared from a museum. The diamond weighed 45 carats and has an estimated value of £8,328,780. How much money is that per carat?

② Detective Ronan is investigating the mystery of the missing diamond. To help solve the mystery, he has decided to review 283 minutes of security video. How many hours and minutes is that?

③ While reviewing the footage, Detective Ronan noticed that the security cameras stopped working at 1:17 AM and resumed filming at 1:24 AM. When the video resumed at 1:24 AM, the diamond was gone. How long were the security cameras not working?

④ Detective Ronan found a hair strand inside the diamond's empty display case. He hopes this hair contains the DNA of the thief. For it to be examined, he needs to get the hair to the forensics laboratory. If he is driving at a speed of 90 km per hour, how long would it take him to get to the laboratory if it's 30 km away from the museum?

⑤ After reviewing security footage a second time, Detective Ronan found that a security officer and two of the janitors were not in their designated locations when the security cameras stopped working. These employees were questioned for a total of 114 minutes. If each person was interviewed separately for an equal amount of time, how many minutes was each person interviewed?

⑥ The three suspects eventually confessed to stealing the diamond and they returned the diamond to the museum. They were also each fined £135,000 for the theft. How much money were the fines of all three thieves combined?

REAL LIFE NUMBERS

# Day 42

Name: ____________________

Score:

**Facts:**

- **Niagara Falls is one of the most famous waterfalls.**
- **Niagara Falls is made from 3 waterfalls: Horseshoe Falls, American Falls, and Bridal Falls**

1. If 2.8 million people visited Niagara Falls in June and 3.5 million visited in July, how many more visitors were there in July?

2. If Niagara Falls produces 2.7 million Kilowatts of energy on the United States side and 2.2 million Kilowatts on the Canadian side, how much energy can it produce all together?

3. A boat drives tourists to the bottom of the falls 16 times each day. If the boat can fit 275 tourists on board, how many people could it bring to the bottom of the falls each day?

**Facts:**

- **Niagara Falls is largest during the day. At night, more water is diverted to produce hydroelectricity.**
- **A teacher named Annie Edson Taylor was the first to go over Niagara Falls while riding inside a barrel.**

4. Horseshoe Falls is the largest section of Niagara Falls. Its crest line is about 2,200 feet long. American Falls has a crest line of 1,050 feet, and Bridal Falls only has a crest line of 50 feet. How many feet of crest line does Niagara Falls have all together?

5. Niagara Falls is 167 feet tall and not even close to being the tallest in the world. Angel Falls is the tallest. It's 3,212 feet tall. How much taller is Angel Falls than Niagara Falls?

6. Victoria Falls is generally considered to be the world's largest waterfall. It's about 360 feet tall and about 5600 feet wide. Knowing that there are 5,280 feet in a mile, how many feet wider is Victoria Falls than a mile?

**Trivia:**

- **Niagara Falls erodes the earth beneath it causing the falls to slowly move upstream. How much does it move each year?**

Name: ____________________

Score:

① Dr. Dale has been an orthopedic surgeon for 24 years. What is the present age of Dr. Dale if she became an orthopedic surgeon at the age of 27?

② Dr. Dale is performing 63 operations this week. If 17 of them are major operations and the rest are minor operations, how many minor operations is she scheduled to perform this week?

③ Dr. Dale's 3rd surgery of the day was scheduled to be from 9:50 AM to 10:25 AM. The surgery did not end until 11:10 AM though. How much longer did this surgery take than scheduled?

④ Dr. Dale has a patient named Kelly. Kelly will need a transfusion of 45 milliliters of blood per hour while his leg is being operated on. If his operation lasts 4 hours, how many milliliters of blood will Kelly receive?

⑤ As the surgery was about to end, Dr. Dale placed stitches on Kelly's leg to close the area where the surgery took place. If it took 20 minutes for the 30 stitches to be placed, on average, how many seconds did it take to place each stitch?

⑥ After the surgery, Dr. Dale advised Kelly to do some leg exercises for 5 minutes a day for a week. For two more weeks thereafter, Kelly was advised to double the time of exercise. How many hours of leg exercising is that during the 3 weeks after his surgery?

Name: ____________________

Score:

**Facts:**

- **Tunnels can be dug by hand, but most are now made with tunnel boring machines.**
- **Boring machines can drill through rocks and soil.**

New York City Subway

① A tunnel boring machine is used to make a subway tunnel. The machine only bores 40 feet of tunnel each day. At this rate, how much tunnel will it bore in a 30-day month?

② The tunnel boring machine has already made a tunnel that is 3,358 feet long but has another 8,662 feet to go. How long will the tunnel be when it is done?

**Facts:**

- **Tunnels are difficult to build but very useful.**
- **They can save time, space, energy, and money.**

③ It used to take Casey 32 minutes to drive to work and 38 minutes to drive back home through traffic. Now the subway can get her to work in 13 minutes and back again in 13 minutes. If Casey works 5 days each week, how much time will the subway save her a week?

④ People ride trains through the Channel Tunnel. If there were 62,167 passengers on Saturday and 55,372 passengers on Sunday, how many passengers were there over the weekend?

**Facts:**

- **The Channel Tunnel passes under the English Channel, connecting England and France by train.**
- **The Seikan Tunnel links Japan's two biggest islands and has the longest stretch of underwater tunnel.**
- **The Delaware Aqueduct is Earth's longest tunnel. It supplies half of New York City's drinking water.**

⑤ The Channel Tunnel is about 31 miles long, the Seikan Tunnel is about 33 miles long, and the Delaware Aqueduct is about 85 miles long. How much longer is the Delaware Aqueduct than the Channel Tunnel and Seikan Tunnel combined?

⑥ If the Delaware Aqueduct's largest diameter is about 19.5 feet and the Channel Tunnel has a diameter of about 25 feet, how much wider is the Channel Tunnel's diameter?

**Trivia:**

- **Some animals can make impressive tunnels too. What mammals are good at digging tunnels?**

Name: ____________________

Score:

1. If a 200 meter race requires swimmers to complete 4 laps in the swimming pool, how many laps would a swimmer need to complete to finish a 500 meter race in the same pool? *(It may help to draw a picture.)*

2. If an Olympic pool can hold about 660,000 gallons of water, how many gallons of water can 5 Olympic size pools hold?

3. Kirsten decided to buy a new swimsuit for £54.37, new goggles for £22.62, and a towel for £9.95. How much money will she need to buy all these items?

4. Kirsten's average time for completing a lap in the pool is 38 seconds. At this rate, how long would it take her to complete 20 laps?

5. There's a total of 145 swimmers in the regional competition. 97 of them are adults and the rest are children. If the registration fee for adults and children is £75 and £58 respectively, how much more does it cost for an adult to register than a child?

6. The first place swimmer in the 1000-meter race finished in 26 minutes and 25 seconds. The second-place swimmer finished after 27 minutes and 8 seconds. What is the difference between the time of the first place and second place swimmers?

# Day 46

Name: ____________________

Score:

**Facts:**

- **People have been dog sledding since ancient times.**
- **They helped people thrive in cold environments.**

① If a dog team's average running speed is 11 miles per hour, how many miles would they be expected to travel after 5 hours of running?

② If each sled dog can pull 85 pounds of weight, how many pounds of weight could a team of 6 dogs pull?

**Facts:**

- **A dog sled team can travel over 100 miles a day.**
- **Siberian huskies and Alaskan malamutes are two of the most common sled dog breeds.**
- **One sled dog can often pull 85 pounds of weight.**

③ If a Siberian husky weighs 55 pound and an Alaskan malamute weighs 90 pounds, how much heavier is the malamute?

④ Dogs use a lot of calories while pulling a sled. If a 55-pound sled dog uses 12,500 calories a day and an adult man only uses 2,500 calories a day, how many times more calories does the sled dog use?

**Facts:**

- **The Iditarod is the most famous dog sled race.**
- **The race begins in Anchorage, Alaska, crosses two mountain ranges, and ends in Nome.**
- **It takes over a week for teams to finish the race.**

⑤ There are two routes that are used for the Iditarod race. It rotates between the north route and the south route. If the north route is 975 miles long and the south route is 998 miles long, how much longer is the south route than the north route?

⑥ The first place sled team took 9 days, 15 hours, and 46 minutes to finish the Iditarod. The second place team took 9 days, 21 hours, and 39 minutes. How much faster was the first place team?

**Trivia:**

- **What is the name of the person that drives a dog sled team?**

Name: ____________________

Score:

1. Bobby wants to buy a new cell phone. The phone costs £799 and its accessories cost £142. How much would he need to pay for the phone and its accessories combined?

2. Bobby's phone has a 32GB storage capacity. If an average app file size is 250MB, how many apps can he download if he wants to use the full storage capacity of his phone? (hint: 1GB = 1,000MB)

3. Bobby observes that an application has an average download time of 2 minutes and 30 seconds. If he wants to download 7 applications, how long will he need to wait for all the applications to be downloaded?

4. A company launches a new update on their application, which will consume 1.4GB of phone storage. Bobby wants to update his phone. The previous update of the application only required 578MB of phone storage. How much additional storage is needed for this application's update?

5. Every minute that Bobby charges his phone, 3% of battery life is being added. If the current battery charge of the phone is 64%, how long would he need to charge his phone in order to return it to a charge of 100%?

6. Bobby plays a game application on his phone that consumes 32 MB of RAM. As he plays, 3 applications are running in the background, which consume 17MB of RAM each. How many MB of RAM do the 4 applications consume together?

# Day 48

Name: ____________________

Score:

**Facts:**

- **A diamond was the hardest known material. Now, some man-made nanomaterials are harder.**
- **Diamonds are measured by their weight. 1 carat is equal to 200 milligrams.**

An Uncut Diamond

1. How many carats would an 800 milligram diamond be?

2. How many milligrams would a 7 carat diamond be?

3. A miner found 66 colorless diamonds, 14 yellow diamonds, and 29 brown diamonds. How many diamonds did the miner find?

**Facts:**

- **Diamonds are not always colorless. They can be yellow, red, blue, pink, purple, black, orange, green, brown, or gray too.**
- **Some colors are more rare and valuable.**
- **Even a 1 carat red diamond can be worth millions of pounds.**

4. To make a diamond look like a jewel, it needs to be cut and polished. If a jeweler starts to cut a diamond at 8:12 AM and doesn't finish polishing it until 3:31 PM, how long did it take the jeweler to finish the diamond? Give your answer in hours and minutes.

5. A jeweler spent £217 on gold and £589 on a diamond to make a diamond ring. She sold that ring for £1,765. How much of a profit did the jeweler make?

**Facts:**

- **Diamonds are used for more than jewelry.**
- **Since they are very hard, diamonds are used to make industrial saws and drills.**
- **They are even used to cut other diamonds.**

6. The largest diamond ever found was 3,106 carats. It was cut into over 100 smaller diamonds, the largest of them weighing 530 carats. How much lighter was the largest cut diamond than the original weight of the diamond?

**Trivia:**

- **What was the largest cut diamond from the largest diamond ever found used for?**

Name: ______________________

Score:

① Coco has a garden that is full of flowers. There are roses, tulips, daffodils, marigolds, daisies, orchids, sunflowers, and carnations. The garden has an equal number of flowers for each type of flower. If the garden has a total of 2,000 flowers, how many roses are in the garden?

② The length of the garden is 4 times its width. If the length of the garden measures 60 meters, what is its width?

③ Coco planted 447 marigold seeds last month. As he checked today, only 382 grew. How many seeds didn't grow?

④ Coco and his employees harvested 18 dozen roses, 15 dozen carnations, 7 dozen marigolds, 5 dozen daisies, and 12 dozen sunflowers. How many flowers did they harvest from the garden?

⑤ Every 5 rows of flowers need 25 liters of water and 70 grams of fertilizer each day. If the garden has 40 rows of flowers, how much fertilizer will be needed each day?

⑥ If the garden's wheelbarrow can carry 35 kilograms of weight at a time, how many wheelbarrow loads will it take to move 700 kilograms of dirt?

Name: ____________

Score:

**Facts:**

- **The sun is the largest object in our solar system.**
- **Roughly a million Earths can fit inside the sun.**
- **The sun is the only star in our solar system.**

1. It takes light from the sun 499 seconds to reach Earth. How long is that in minutes and seconds?

2. Mars is farther from the sun than Earth. If it takes sunlight 761 seconds to reach Mars, how much longer does it take to reach Mars than Earth? *(Use information from question 1)*

3. How much hotter is the center of the sun than the surface of the sun? *(Use information from the Facts box)*

**Facts:**

- **The sun's gravity is so strong it makes hydrogen atoms fuse together.**
- **This process is called nuclear fusion, and it allows the sun to create a lot of heat.**
- **The surface of the sun is about 6,000 °C, and the center of the sun is 15,000,000 °C.**

4. If the sun travels along its orbit at a speed of about 217 km every second, how far does the sun travel in a minute?

5. Scientists believe the sun has enough fuel to burn for 5 billion more years. If this is true, how old will the sun be when it runs out of fuel? *(Use information from the Facts box)*

**Facts:**

- **Scientists believe the sun is 4.6 billion years old.**
- **The sun orbits the center of the Milky Way Galaxy and completes one orbit every 230 million years.**

6. The closest solar system to ours is Alpha Centauri. It's about 4.37 light years from Earth. The next closest star is called Barnard's Star, and it's about 5.96 light years away. How much closer to Earth is Alpha Centauri than Barnard's Star?

**Trivia:**

- **How many stars are in the Alpha Centauri solar system?**

# Day 51

Name: ____________________

Score:

① 5,341 buildings were damaged in a recent earthquake, but only 615 of these buildings sustained major damages. The rest only had minor damages. How many buildings had minor damages?

② The city estimates that 43 roads will also need to be repaired after the earthquake. If it will cost £2,450 to repair each of these roads, how much should the city plan to spend on these road repairs?

③ Mark's home had 6 of its windows break during the earthquake. It cost him £552 to replace these windows. How much money was that per window?

④ 20,010 homes lost power during the earthquake. Two days later, 8,443 homes were still waiting for their electricity to be restored. How many homes had their electricity restored?

⑤ Rachel is an electrical technician. Normally, she works 40 hours a week. But the week of the earthquake, she worked 65 hours to help restore power throughout the city. If she was paid £48.50 per hour for the extra hours she worked that week, how much extra money did she make that week?

⑥ Jeremy owns a hardware store. His store normally sells £35,000 worth of hardware a week. But the week of the earthquake, the store's sales quadrupled. What were his sales the week of the earthquake?

Name: ____________________

Score:

**Facts:**

- **Salmon live most of their lives in the ocean, then swim up rivers by the millions to spawn and lay eggs.**
- **Some travel thousands of km upstream to spawn.**

① Researchers estimate that 54.8 million sockeye salmon and 35.2 million pink salmon will swim up a river to spawn. How many salmon is that all together?

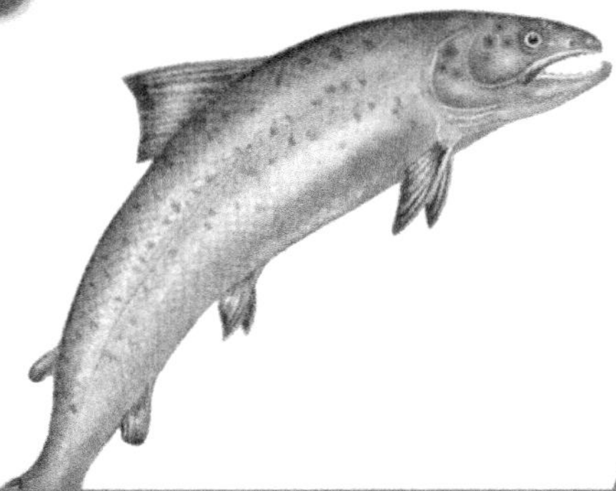

② One salmon lays 2,045 eggs, another salmon lays 3,856 eggs. How many eggs is that total?

**Facts:**

- **Salmon are keystone species because their ecosystem's existence largely depends on them.**
- **Bears, eagles, killer whales, and over a hundred other animals rely on salmon for food.**

③ Six brown bears are standing in a river trying to catch salmon as they swim upstream. If each bear catches 13 salmon, how many will the bears catch all together?

**Facts:**

- **Dams produce clean electricity, but block rivers making it hard for salmon to swim upstream.**
- **Newly hatched salmon often die trying to swim through dam turbines to get down river.**
- **Fish ladders let fish swim around dams instead.**

④ 87,310 newly hatched salmon passed through a dam turbine today, but only 34,793 survived. How many did not survive?

⑤ Lisa counted salmon as they swam up a fish ladder. She counted 45 salmon in 5 minutes. How many salmon is that per minute?

⑥ A salmon bit a hook at 10:48 AM. It took the fisherman 24 minutes to reel it in, take a picture, and release it back into the water. What time was the fish released?

**Trivia:**

- **What do people call an up-stream migration of salmon?**

Name: ___________________

Score:

① James was one of the knights in the queen's palace. He started his training when he was 7 years old and became a knight 16 years later. How old was James when he became a knight?

② The knight's metal armor weighs 45 pounds. If James weighs 204 pounds while wearing this armor, how much does he weigh without the armor?

③ A knight wears a linen shirt under his armor. If it takes 3 yards of linen to make 2 shirts, how many shirts can be made from 120 yards of linen?

④ The knight's shield is 3 times heavier than his sword. If his sword weighs 14 pounds, how heavy is his shield?

⑤ The sword of a knight needs to be sharpened using 5 mL of oil 3 times a week. How much oil is that each month? (Estimate that a month is 4 weeks long.)

⑥ James practices sword fighting an hour and a half every morning and an hour each evening. How much practice is that each week?

Name: ____________________

Score:

**Facts:**

- **Antarctica is the fifth largest continent. It's larger than Europe and almost twice as large as Australia.**
- **Antarctica is the coldest, driest, & windiest continent.**

(1) Antarctica's mainland was first seen by a ship in 1820. Explorers traveled inland and reached the South Pole 91 years later. What year did they reach the South Pole?

(2) It takes wind speeds of 119 km per hour to be considered "hurricane strength winds." Antarctica often has winds over 160 km per hour. How much faster is that than hurricane strength winds?

(3) With a rate of half a centimeter of precipitation a year, how many years would it take to receive a total of 7 centimeters of precipitation?

**Facts:**

- **The Antarctic desert is the largest desert on Earth.**
- **Antarctica's interior only gets about half a centimeter of precipitation a year.**

(4) Antarctica has the world's coldest temperatures. Thermometers on the ground have measured temperatures as low as –89 °C. Satellite instruments have measured temperatures of –98 °C. How much colder is the satellite measurement?

**Facts:**

- **Antarctica has 90% of the world's ice.**
- **Its ice sheets can be nearly 5 km thick and took millions of years to form.**

(5) More people visit Antarctica each year. If 72,503 tourists went to Antarctica last year and 56,398 went the year before that, how many more tourists were there last year than the year before?

(6) Most people visit Antarctica during its warmer summer months. Antarctica's summer happens while the Northern Hemisphere is having winter. That's why only 3,400 people visited Antarctica during July, and eight times as many people visited in January. How many visited in January?

**Trivia:**

- **Most animals leave Antarctica's mainland during the winter. Only one warm-blooded animal stays. What animal is it?**

Name: ____________________

Score:

① The tallest lighthouse in the world is located in Saudi Arabia and is 436 feet tall. The second tallest lighthouse is located in the state of Ohio and is 352 feet tall. How much taller is the lighthouse in Saudi Arabia than the one in Ohio?

② If the lighthouse builders work on making the foundation for 36 days, the body of the tower for 59 days, the staircases for 45 days, the control room for 12 days, and the watch room for 15 days, how long would it take the builders to finish the lighthouse?

③ The lighthouse keeper uses 2 gallons of fuel per month to light the torch. How many gallons of fuel are needed to light the torch of the lighthouse per year?

④ The lighthouse builders decided to build lighthouses that are 35 miles apart. How many lighthouses will there be if the shoreline is 4,900 miles long?

⑤ One of the lighthouses stopped working shortly after it was built. If it cost £1,782 to buy a new light bulb and £325 to install the new bulb, how much money did it cost to repair the lighthouse?

⑥ From 1886 to 1901, the Statue of Liberty functioned as a lighthouse that helped boats navigate New York Harbor. How many years was it used as a lighthouse?

# Day 56

Name: ____________________

Score:

**Facts:**

- **Maple sap is mostly water. It looks like water too.**
- **The sap is boiled to evaporate most of the water, leaving behind a small amount sweet maple syrup.**

**Facts:**

- **Many people in Canada refer to maple syrup as "liquid gold."**
- **Quebec produces about 70% of the world's supply of maple syrup.**
- **Modern maple farmers use suction pumps and tubes to collect sap from the trees more efficiently.**
- **Maple syrup is mostly made of sugar, but it also contains many minerals and antioxidants too.**

1. If 40 gallons of sap is needed to produce a gallon of maple syrup, how many gallons of sap would be needed to make 4 gallons of syrup?

2. Isabell is collecting sap from 9 different trees. If each tree produces 15 gallons of sap, how many gallons of sap will she have all together?

3. One gallon of sap weighs about 8 pounds. Isabell stores her sap in 5-gallon buckets. How much weight is Isabell lifting when she carries 2 full 5-gallon buckets of sap?

4. Isabell boils her sap in 10-gallon batches. If it takes 4 hours to boil one batch of sap, how much time will it take her to boil 30 gallons of sap?

5. Isabell sells her maple syrup for 20 pounds a jar. If she sells 30 jars over the weekend, how much money will she have made?

6. Isabell has been making syrup for 3 years now. If she made £840 the first year, £780 the second year, and £1,060 the third year, how much money has she made?

**Trivia:**

- **How can you tell if maple syrup is real or fake?**

Name: ______________________

Score:

① The average number of players on a basketball team is 15. If there's a total of 20 teams competing for the playoffs, how many players are there in all?

② Team Bumble Bees scored 24 points less than Team Lions.
If Team Lions' score was 87, what was the score of Team Bumble Bees?

③ Team Grizzlies scored 27 points in the first quarter, 35 in the second quarter, 28 in the third quarter, and 17 in the fourth quarter. What is the team's total score?

④ Team Lions won the championship this season. They will be receiving a cash prize of £600. If the team has a total of 15 players, how much will each player receive?

⑤ There was 1 minute and 7 seconds left in the game. Team Lions then had the ball for 22 seconds before a timeout was called. How much time is left in the game now?

⑥ The width of the tournament's basketball court is half its length. If the width is 48 feet, how long is the basketball court? (It may help to draw a picture.)

# Day 58

Name: ____________________

Score:

**Facts:**

- **The Amazon Rainforest is Earth's largest rainforest.**
- **It's roughly the size of the USA's lower 48 states.**

① It rains about 8 feet 6 inches each year in some parts of the Amazon Rainforest. If it rained 8 feet 6 inches last year and 7 feet 8 inches the year before that, how many more inches did it rain last year than the year before?

② During the dry season, the Amazon River is often 6 miles wide, but during the rainy season it can become 24 miles wide. How many times wider is the Amazon River during the rainy season?

**Facts:**

- **The Amazon Rainforest has millions of plant and animal species, making it the most biodiverse place on Earth.**
- **Hundreds of new species are discovered each year.**

③ Marco drives people up the Amazon River in his boat. If he drove 7 hours today and traveled 287 miles up the river, how many miles per hour did his boat travel?

④ Researchers disagree on the exact length of the Amazon River, but most agree that it is over 4000 miles long. How much shorter is the Mississippi River if the Mississippi is about 2,320 miles long?

**Facts:**

- **Large areas of the Amazon Rainforest are being cut down or burned to make room for farms and cattle pastures.**
- **Thousands of species are going extinct because of this.**

⑤ If about 70 square miles of the Amazon's rainforest is being cleared each week, roughly how many square miles will be cleared in four weeks?

⑥ If 3,245 square miles of rainforest were cleared one year and 3,819 were cleared the next, how many square miles were cleared during both years combined?

**Trivia:**

- **How many bridges cross the Amazon River?**

# Day 59

Name: ____________________

Score:

1. There has been a major drought this year. To conserve water, the city of Clarksville has placed water restrictions on 14,637 homes, and the city of Mayfield has placed water restrictions on 8,521 homes. Between the two cities, how many homes were placed on water restrictions?

2. The town of Clarksville saved 593 cubic meters of water in its water tank for drought season. The town already consumed 372 cubic meters of this water during the last 2 months. How much water is left in the tank?

3. If a family consumes three and a half cubic meters of water per week, how much water will they consume in 4 weeks?

4. During a normal year, a farmer can harvest 70 bags of grain from her field. During this year's drought, she was only able to harvest 43 bags of grain from her field. How many fewer bags of grain is that?

5. The farmer harvested 28 pounds of strawberries and sold them for £9 a pound. She also harvested 54 pounds of cherries and sold them for £6 per pound. How much money did she make from her strawberry and cherry harvests combined?

6. The farmer harvested 550 pounds of beans last year and sold them for £2 per pound. This year she only harvested 270 pounds of beans but was able to sell them for £3 a pound. How much more money was made from the bean harvest last year than this year?

# Day 60

Name: ____________________

Score:

**Facts:**

- **Blue whales are the largest animals to ever live. They're larger than any of the dinosaurs were.**
- **Blue whales can weigh as much as 30 elephants.**

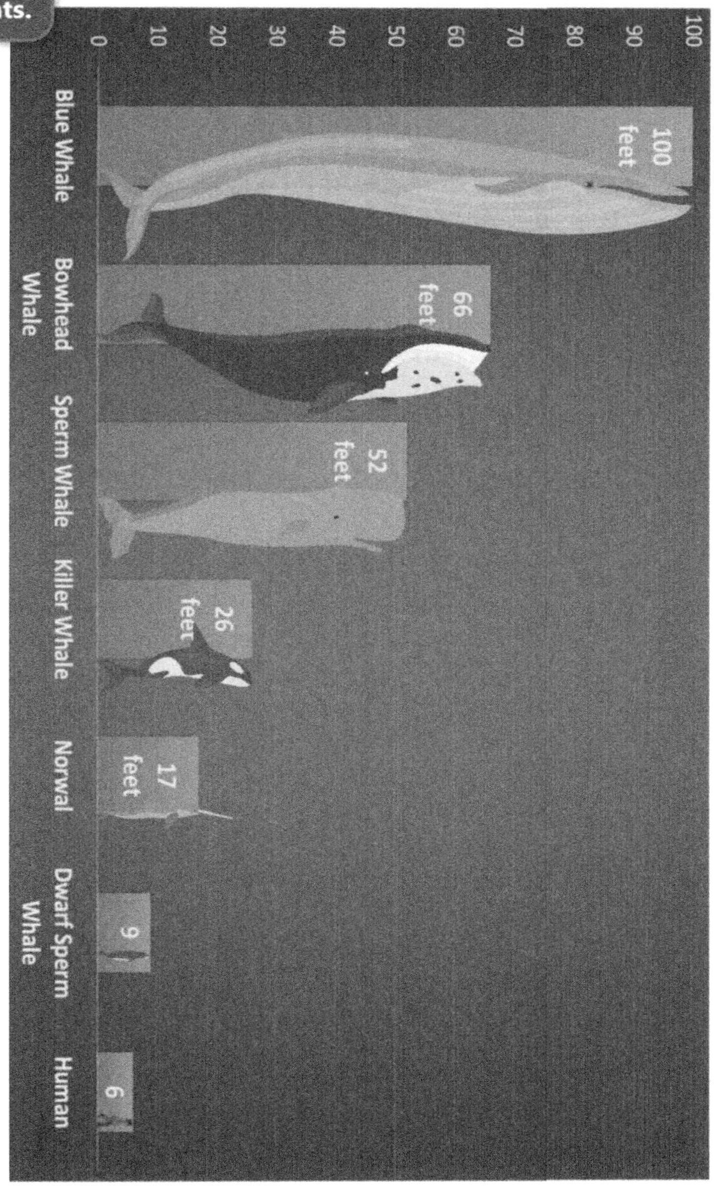


① How much longer is a blue whale than a sperm whale?

② Blue whales have a massive appetite. They eat millions of tiny creatures called krill each day. If one whale eats 32 million krill, a second eats 44 million krill, and a third eats 35 million krill, how many krill did they eat together?

③ A blue whale is about 25 feet long when it is born and can weigh over 8,000 pounds. If the average car weighs about 4,000 pounds, roughly how many cars would it take to equal the weight of a newborn blue whale?

④ Baby blue whales grow fast. They gain about 200 pounds each day. At this rate, how many days would it take an 8,000-pound baby to weigh 10,000 pounds?

⑤ A killer whale is not a whale. Killer whales, also known as orcas, are the world's largest species of dolphin. Roughly how many orcas would it take to equal the length of one blue whale?

**Facts:**

- **Bowhead whales can live to be over 200 years old, making them the longest living mammal we know of.**
- **Other whale species have very long lives too.**

⑥ Not all whales are huge. The dwarf sperm whale is the world's smallest whale species. They're about 9 feet long and weigh 500 pounds when fully grown. How many dwarf sperm whales would it take to weigh as much as an 8,000-pound baby blue whale?

**Trivia:**

- **How far can a whale's song travel underwater?**

Name: ____________________

Score:

① Bruce has worked as a helicopter pilot for an aviation company for 12 years. His present age is four times his years of service in the company. How old is Bruce?

② Bruce took 2 hours and 30 minutes to fly the helicopter from Glasgow to London. The distance between the two cities is about 350 miles. What was the helicopter's average speed? *(State your answer in miles per hour.)*

③ After the flight, Bruce's helicopter only has 46 liters of fuel left in its tank, but it's capable of holding 180 liters of fuel. If helicopter fuel costs £3 a liter, how much money will Bruce need to fill the tank back up again?

④ Bruce notices that the helicopter engine isn't running right. New parts for the engine are going to cost £250. Bruce will also need to pay a mechanic £120 to replace these parts, as well as a £75 maintenance fee that the repair shop charges. How much money is that all together?

⑤ The helicopter uses an average of 160 liters of fuel during an 8-hour flight. If a liter of fuel costs £3, how much would it cost Bruce to take a 5-hour flight?

⑥ Bruce also works as a flight instructor. This allows him to earn an extra £3,400 every month. If his monthly salary as a pilot is £8,500, how much does Bruce make a year by working both of these jobs?

# Day 62

Name: ____________________

Score:

**Facts:**

- **Pigeons may have been the first domesticated bird.**
- **They probably shared caves with ancient humans.**

(1) There are 14 pigeon nests under a bridge. If 9 of the nests have 2 eggs, 3 of the nests have 1 egg, and 2 of the nests have 3 eggs, how many pigeon eggs are there under the bridge?

**Facts:**

- **Pigeons are clever. They can recognize people in photographs and learn the letters of the alphabet.**
- **If a pigeon is taken hundreds of miles from its home and released, it will often find its way back again.**
- **People used to tie written notes to a pigeon's leg and release it so that the pigeon would return to their home and carry the message with them.**
- **Messenger Pigeons were used for thousands of years and were the fastest form of communication.**

(2) Many people don't like pigeons because of all the poop they drop. But years ago, their poop was prized and collected for fertilizer. If 4 pounds of pigeon poop was worth 20 copper coins, how many copper coins was that for each pound of pigeon poop?

(3) Ralph raises pigeons. If one bag of bird food can feed his pigeons for 7 weeks, how many weeks can 3 bags of bird food feed his pigeons?

(4) Each bag of bird seed costs 9 pounds. If Ralph is buying 3 bags of bird seed and gives the store clerk 2 twenty-pound notes, how much change should Ralph expect to get back?

(5) A messenger pigeon from Chicago was released in Washington D.C. This pigeon flew non-stop for 600 miles back to its home in Chicago. If the pigeon's average flight speed was 60 miles per hour, how many hours did it take the pigeon to complete the journey?

(6) Pigeons can fly 60 miles per hour for long distances but are able to fly 100 miles per hour for short distances. How much faster is their fastest flying speed than their long-distance flying speed?

**Trivia:**

- **Why are many pigeons considered war heroes and awarded medals of honor?**

Name: ____________________

Score:

(1) The Lito family is having a family reunion this year. The last family reunion was 10 years ago and they had 348 people attend. This year's reunion is supposed to have 63 more people attend. How many people are expected to attend this year's reunion?

(2) It will cost £7.00 for every adult meal served at the reunion and £4.50 for every children's meal served. If 274 adults ordered a meal and 98 children ordered a meal, how much will the food for these meals cost?

(3) 6 cakes were also ordered for the meal. If the 6 cakes together can serve 330 people, how many people could each cake serve?

(4) The Lito family hired a band to play music during their party. If the band started playing music at 5:45 PM and were hired to play music for three and a half hours, what time should the band stop playing?

(5) Margretta was in charge of organizing the family reunion. She was given a budget of £3,000 to set up the accommodations. If the band costs £950, the building the reunion was held in costs £1,400, and the decorations for the reunion costs £285, how much under budget was Margretta?

(6) Thomas' family drove 115 miles to be at the reunion. Bethany's family flew six times as far to attend the reunion. How far did Bethany's family travel?

Name: ____________________

Score:

**Facts:**

- **92% of a watermelon's weight is water.**
- **Watermelons originated in Southern Africa and were cherished by those trying to cross the Kalahari Desert.**
- **They were sometimes left in the tombs of Egyptian kings as a form of nourishment in the afterlife.**

1. Bri carried two watermelons to her car. One was 37 pounds, the other 34 pounds. A store worker carried a third, which weighed 41 pounds. How much more weight did Bri carry than the worker?

2. Bri collected 357 seeds from one watermelon, 582 seeds from another, and 446 seeds from a third melon. How many seeds does she have?

**Facts:**

- **You can eat the whole watermelon.**
- **The green-white rinds are cooked and eaten in many cultures.**
- **Seeds can be eaten raw or roasted.**
- **Lycopene is what makes the flesh pink. This nutrient is believed to reduce the rate of many cancers. (It also makes tomatoes red.)**

3. Bri is going to roast 2 batches of seeds. If each batch takes 20 minutes to roast and she starts roasting at 9:46 AM, what time will the last batch be done?

4. If 1 cup of watermelon has 8 mg of lycopene and 1 cup of raw tomatoes has 5.5 mg of lycopene, how much more lycopene does the cup of watermelon have?

**Facts:**

- **There are over 1,200 varieties of watermelons.**
- **Their insides are not always pink. They can have orange, green, yellow, or white insides.**
- **Glass containers can be placed around the melons as they grow to make them different shapes, such as cubes, hearts, and pyramids.**

5. Cube shaped watermelons often cost £300, when a regular watermelon only costs £6. At these prices, how many regular watermelons could you buy for the price of one cube shaped watermelon?

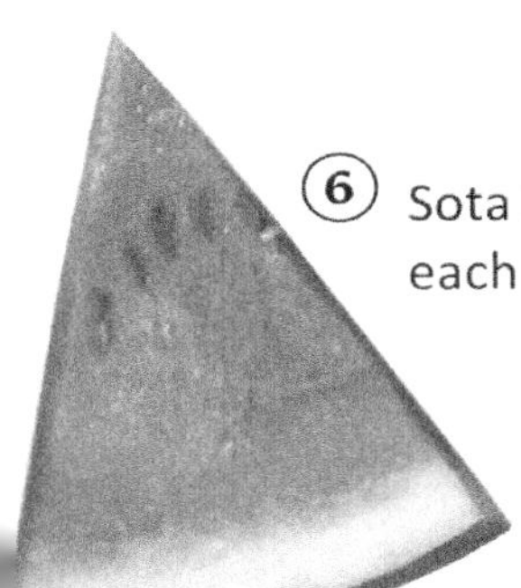

6. Sota is a watermelon farmer. He recently sold 250 cube shaped watermelons for £300 each and 1,400 regular watermelons for £6 each. How much money did Sota make?

**Trivia:**

- **How much did the heaviest watermelon weigh?**

Name: ____________________

Score:

1. Ralph really wants to go to a theme park, but his parents say that he will need to buy his own ticket. One ticket to enter the park is £34 and Ralph currently has £7. If he earns £4 a week for doing chores and saves all this money for the ticket, how many weeks will it be before he has enough money for the ticket?

2. Ralph doesn't want to wait that long, so he finds babysitting jobs to earn extra money. If he earned £5 from his first babysitting job and £3 more than that from his second babysitting job, how much money did he earn from these two jobs combined?

3. Ralph finally saved enough for the ticket. His parents were proud of how hard he worked for the money. So, they decided to reward him with £7 of spending money at the theme park. If Ralph used this money to buy a hotdog for £4.85 and a soda for £1.50, how much of the £7 is left over?

4. Ralph's favorite ride is the red roller coaster. He rode this roller coaster 7 times and had to wait in line 13 minutes each time. How much time did he spend waiting in line for this roller coaster?

5. Ralph is currently in line for the red roller coaster. 67 people are still in front of him. If the roller coaster has 8 cars and each car seats 2 people each time it runs, how many more times will the roller coaster need to run before Ralph gets a seat on one of the cars?

6. The theme park is going to stop running the rides at 9:00 PM. It is currently 7:48 PM. If Ralph can ride the Farris wheel once every 9 minutes, how many times will he be able to ride the Farris wheel before the rides stop running?

# Day 66

Name: ____________________

Score:

**Facts:**

- **Mosquitoes may be the world's most dangerous animal.**
- **They often spread diseases to people. These mosquito-borne illnesses kill over a million people a year.**

**Facts:**

- **There are about 3,500 different species of mosquitoes, but most do not bite humans.**
- **Some mosquito species prefer the blood of particular animals, perhaps choosing to bite cattle over humans or only targeting birds.**

① A city had 56 cases of malaria in July. If that's exactly 7 times more cases of malaria than June, how many malaria cases did the city have in June?

② If 230 million people contracted malaria last year and 407,000 of these people did not survive, how many of these people did survive?

③ Roger played outside for 2 hours and received 12 mosquito bites during that time. On average, how many mosquito bites was that per hour?

④ Mosquitoes can live to be 6 months old. Roughly how many days old is that?
*(Hint: Estimate that there are 30 days in a month.)*

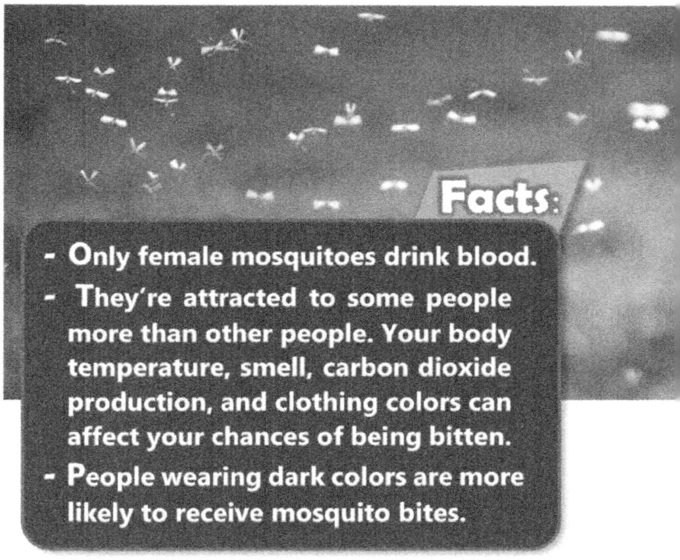

**Facts:**

- **Only female mosquitoes drink blood.**
- **They're attracted to some people more than other people. Your body temperature, smell, carbon dioxide production, and clothing colors can affect your chances of being bitten.**
- **People wearing dark colors are more likely to receive mosquito bites.**

⑤ Mosquitoes beat their wings so quickly it creates a buzzing sound. If a mosquito is beating its wings 300 times a second, how long would it take for this mosquito to beat its wings 4,500 times?

⑥ Mosquitoes may beat their wings fast, but they do not travel very fast. If a mosquito can travel 1.5 miles per hour, how many miles could it travel in 4 hours?

**Trivia:**

- **If only female mosquitoes suck blood, what do male mosquitoes eat?**

# Day 67

Name: ____________________

Score:

① Each mountain climber needs to pay a £12.80 environmental fee before they can start climbing the mountain. If there are 35 mountain climbers, how much do they need to pay for the environmental fee in total?

② Following the protocols, they need a tour guide for every 5 mountain climbers. If there are 35 mountain climbers, how many tour guides do they need?

③ This will be Peter's first time climbing a mountain. Due to his excitement, he went to an outdoor gear shop and bought a new compass worth £45, a rope for £12, a flashlight for £23, and a tent for £175. How much did he need to pay for it all?

④ The height of the mountain that they need to climb is 9,561 feet. As they reached the last campsite, Peter checked his map and told his co-climbers that they were already at an elevation of 7,693 feet. How much higher do they need to climb to reach the top of the mountain?

⑤ The trail from the last campsite to the peak is 8 miles long. If it took them 2 hours and 56 minutes to complete this hike, on average, how many minutes did it take to hike each mile?

⑥ During the climb up the mountain, Peter saw 3 bears and 45 mountain goats. How many mountain goats did he see for every bear?

# REAL LIFE NUMBERS

# Day 68

**Facts:**

- **Solar energy can make electricity without pollution.**
- **Solar energy may be the cheapest form of electricity.**

Name: ______________________

Score:

① Flora installed 12 solar panels on her roof. Each panel is supposed to produce 300 watts per hour in direct sunlight. If there is direct sunlight for about 5 hours per day, how many watts of energy should these panels produce a day?

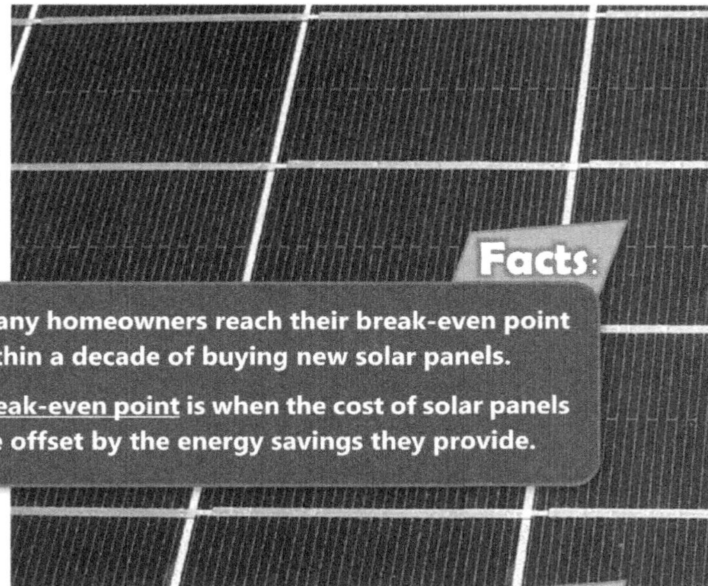

② After a month, Flora's panels have collected dust, which blocks some of the sunlight. Now the 12 panels only produce 5,364 watts per hour. How many watts per hour is that per panel?

**Facts:**

- **Many homeowners reach their break-even point within a decade of buying new solar panels.**
- **<u>Break-even point</u> is when the cost of solar panels are offset by the energy savings they provide.**

③ Flora is pleased with her solar panels, so she buys 8 more. If each panel costs £935, how much did she pay for the 8 panels?

④ If one solar panel is 3 feet by 5 feet, how many square feet of area will 8 solar panels cover?

**Facts:**

- **Solar energy is typically the most reliable form of electricity in outer space.**
- **Solar panels provide satellites and Martian land rovers the energy they need to operate.**

⑤ Flora estimates that each panel will save her £85 a year in energy expenses. At this rate, how many years will it take a panel to offset its £935 cost?

⑥ If each solar panel saves Flora £85 worth of energy expenses a year, how much will all 20 save her a year?

**Trivia:**

- **How many square feet of solar panels does the International Space Station have?**

Name: ____________________

Score:

① Brent is a regular customer in the pet shop. He always gets a £5 discount on every sack of cat food he buys. How much would his total discount be if he buys 12 sacks of cat food?

② Eight fish were sold yesterday, and an additional seven fish were sold today. If there are 26 fish left in the aquarium, how many fish were there initially?

③ Each hamster at the pet shop is fed 12 pellets of hamster food a day. If the pet shop has 28 hamsters, how many pellets will the hamsters eat each day?

④ The pet shop has 32 parrots. If there are 2 parrots in each cage, how many parrot cages does the pet shop have?

⑤ The pet shop has 3 times as many snakes as they have turtles. If the pet shop has 8 turtles, how many snakes does it have?

⑥ Kevin fell in love with a Pomeranian dog in the pet shop and bought it for £450. He also bought 4 sacks of dog food for £25 each and a dog food bowl for £8.49. How much would his change be if he gives the clerk £600 for these items?

Name: ______________________

Score:

**Facts:**

- **Rattlesnakes use their tongue to taste the air and sense vibrations in the ground.**
- **Heat-sensitive pits also give them a sort of infrared vision to find prey in the dark.**

(1) A rattlesnake vibrates its rattle about 90 times a second to make its iconic rattling sound to warn predators away. How many times is that in a minute?

(2) A baby rattle snake is born with one rattle. If it sheds its skin every 3 months, how long would it take this rattlesnake to grow 6 more rattles? *(Use information from the Facts box.)*

**Facts:**

- **They prefer to hide when threats are near.**
- **If they can't hide, they shake their tail to warn predators away. Biting is a last resort.**
- **Their rattles are made of keratin, the same substance human hair and nails are made of.**
- **Each time a rattlesnake sheds its skin, an extra segment is added to its rattle.**
- **Rattles are fragile and periodically break off.**

(3) Rattlesnakes can live to be 20 years old. If one sheds its skin about every 3 months, how many times will it shed its skin in 20 years?

(4) Allen was looking at a 44-inch rattlesnake at the zoo, when a zookeeper told him that some rattlesnakes grow to be 7 feet long. How much longer is that than the one Allen was looking at?

(5) If there are about 7,500 rattlesnake bites in the United States each year, but only about 5 of those people die because of the bite, how many people in the U.S. would you expect to be bitten by a rattlesnake each decade?

(6) Rattlesnake venom is used to make antivenom. "Snake milkers" collect snake venom and sell the venom to companies that make the antivenom. If a snake milker collected 6 grams of venom and sold the venom for £1,740 per gram, how much money did this snake milker make?

**Trivia:**

- **Why is it dangerous for people when a rattlesnake's rattle breaks off?**

Name: ____________________

Score:

(1) Levi and his 4 friends are heading to the train station. If each train ticket costs £17 and Levi is in charge of purchasing all of their tickets, how much money will Levi need?

(2) There are 28 ticketing machines in the train station. If 3 of them are having some technical issues and 2 are offline, how many ticketing machines are working properly?

(3) The train is running at an average speed of 120 km per hour. If Levi and his friends' destination is 420 km away, how long will it take them to get there?

(4) The railroad company requires all the engines in every train to have its oil changed every 92 days. If the train Levi is riding had its oil changed 76 days ago, how many more days can pass before it will be due for an oil change again?

(5) There are a total of 4 track inspectors assigned to check a 680-km length of track. If each of these inspectors checks a section of the track that is equal to the other inspectors, how many km of track will each track inspector inspect?

(6) One track inspector noticed a problem with a section of the track and will not permit trains to pass until the problem is fixed. The company estimates that it will take a week to fix the problem and that they will lose £2,730 each day the trains are not able to use this section of track. How much money does the company expect to lose while the problem is being fixed?

Name: ____________________

Score:

**Facts:**

- **Most caves are created by water. Water can slowly dissolve limestone, similar to how it dissolves sugar.**
- **Cracks and gaps form in the stone, creating caves.**

① Tyler is a cave explorer. If he entered a cave at 8:17 AM and did not leave the cave until 3:42 PM, how much time did he spend in the cave?

② The largest cave chamber Tyler found was 9.03 meters tall. The second largest chamber was 5.74 meters tall. How much taller was the largest chamber?

**Facts:**

- **As water dissolves stone in some places, it can deposit minerals in other places.**
- **Water dripping from a cave ceiling can slowly form a stalactite, which looks a lot like an icicle, even though it's a stone.**

③ Tyler found a stalactite that was 1.24 meters long. If this stalactite grows an average of 2 cm longer every 100 years, how old would this stalactite be? *(Hint: there are 100 cm in a meter.)*

④ Tyler moves slowly through caves, so he does not damage any of their cave formations. If he only explores about 400 feet of cave an hour, how many hours will it take to explore a cave that is 3,000 feet long?

**Facts:**

- **Many animals live in caves. Some species are only found inside caves.**
- **Some cave animals have evolved to have no eyes and transparent skin.**
- **Humans have used caves for shelter for thousands of years.**

⑤ Tyler had to rappel down a rope 54 feet to reach the bottom of a cavern. If he made it to the bottom in 18 seconds, what was the speed of his descent down the rope? *(Hint: State your answer in feet per second.)*

⑥ Archeologists found a saber-toothed-cat skull in a cave and believe it is about 29,500 years old. Ancient people also made paintings in the cave. These paintings are believed to be 12,700 years old. If true, how much older is the cat skull than the paintings?

**Trivia:**

- **What is the world's longest known cave system?**

Name: ____________________

Score:

① The length of a pirate ship is five times its width.
How wide is the pirate ship if the length is 325 feet?

② The pirates had started their expedition to find a lost city that was believed to contain a lot of gold. Based on the map, it is 2,520 miles away. The pirate captain tells his crew that it will take 9 days for them to sail there. How many miles a day is that?

③ The pirate ship is passing through a sea where the climate is very hot.
If the crew drinks 3 barrels of water a day, how many barrels of water will they use during their 9-day journey?

④ The jolly roger flag was located 6 feet above the crow's nest. How high above the deck was the flag if the crow's nest was 19 feet above the deck of the pirate ship?

⑤ Pirates found 7 treasure chests that contained 35 gems and 96 gold coins each.
How many gems is that?

⑥ The pirates want to split the gold coins evenly amongst the crew members.
If there are 16 crew members, how many gold coins should each member receive?
*(Use the information from question 5 to answer this question.)*

# Day 74

Name: ____________________

Score:

**Facts:**

- **Corn originally only grew in the Americas but is now farmed on every continent except Antarctica.**
- **Native Americans cultivated many varieties of corn and often traded it like money for other goods.**

(1) If an average ear of corn has 800 kernels, roughly how many kernels would 25 ears of corn have?

(2) Abigail harvests 12 rows of corn each time she drives her combine across her corn field. At this rate, how many times would she need to cross the corn field to harvest 60 rows of corn?

**Facts:**

- **The United States and China are the top corn producing countries.**
- **More U.S. corn is used to feed livestock than to feed people.**

(3) Abigail's cow herd eats about 1,200 pounds of corn a day. How many pounds of corn is that each month? *(Estimate that a month contains 30 days)*

**Facts:**

- **Corn starches can be used to make sweeteners, such as corn syrup.**
- **These sweeteners are often included in foods like bread, crackers, candy, ketchup, fruit drinks, and sodas.**
- **Look at the foods in your home. How many list corn syrup or high-fructose corn syrup as an ingredient?**

*A spoon pouring corn syrup.*

(4) If the United States produced 14,163 million bushels of corn last year and China produced 10,258 million bushels of corn, how much more corn did the United States produce?

(5) If it takes 1 bushel of corn to sweeten 400 cans of soda, how many bushels of corn would it take to sweeten 2,000 cans of soda?

(6) If 5 cups of corn syrup are needed to make 45 caramel candies, how many caramel candies could 1 cup of corn syrup make?

**Trivia:**

- **Why do many healthcare experts recommend limiting the amount of corn sweeteners you eat?**

Name: ____________________

Score:

① Zyrus has 76 science problems to finish for school. If these 76 problems are broken into 4 equal sections, how many problems are there in each section?

② Zyrus completed 6 problems in his English homework. If he needs to answer 14 more problems, how many English problems did his homework have all together?

③ Zyrus did not finish the science problems over the weekend. Now school starts in an hour and a half, and he still has 30 problems to finish. How many minutes is that per problem before school starts?

④ 4 paper pieces are needed for his art project. If Zyrus can finish one paper piece in 7 minutes, how long will it take him to finish all the paper pieces needed?

⑤ Zyrus has his homework in mathematics that is composed of 5 easy, 3 average, and 2 difficult questions. If he can finish answering an easy question in 25 seconds, an average question in 1 minute and 10 seconds, and a difficult question in 4 minutes and 45 seconds, how long will it take him to finish his homework?
(*State your answer in minutes and seconds.*)

⑥ Zyrus needs to get 450 points out of 500 points in his mathematics class to earn an "A." So far, he has earned 387 points. How many more points does he need to earn to get an "A"?

# Day 76

Name: ____________________

Score:

**Facts:**

- **A healthy hen can lay about 265 eggs a year.**
- **Chicken eggs can be white, brown, blue, green, and pink colored.**

**Facts:**

- **Younger hens lay smaller eggs.**
- **Egg shells are mainly made of calcium carbonate.**
- **Egg shells mixed in garden soil will decompose and become fertilizer.**

① Mr. Tinson harvested a total of 15,670 chicken eggs last year. This year, he had a farm expansion and harvested five times as much as he had last year. How many chicken eggs did he harvest this year?

② There are a total of 480 hens on Mr. Tinson's farm. If each hen lays an average of 265 eggs each year, how many trays of eggs can they produce annually if each tray holds 30 eggs?

③ Out of 328 chicken eggs produced, only 297 passed the quality control procedure. How many chicken eggs were defective?

④ If the average egg contains 70 calories, how many calories are in 6 eggs?

⑤ The farmers harvested 521 small eggs, 759 medium eggs, and 378 large eggs yesterday. If they harvested 312 small eggs, 267 medium eggs, and 175 large eggs today, how many eggs did they harvest all together?

⑥ Michelle needs to buy eggs for her bakery. She has a budget of 21 pounds for the eggs. How many dozens of eggs can she buy if each dozen eggs costs £1.59?

**Trivia:**

- **How old is a chicken when it first starts to lay eggs?**

# Day 77

Name: ____________________

Score:

1. Megan works as a garbage collector in a waste management company. Her annual salary is £42,000. How much is that per month?

2. Megan lifts an average of 8,460 kg of garbage every day. How much garbage does Megan lift a week if she works 5 days a week?

3. Megan starts working at 8:00 in the morning and ends at 4:00 in the afternoon. How many hours does she work each day?

4. Megan and her partner collected 26 more trash bins today than they collected yesterday. If they collected 1,765 trash bins today, how many trash bins did they collect yesterday?

5. After collecting all the garbage in the areas assigned to them, part of their job is to go to the transfer stations to deliver all the waste they collected. Every hour, 12 garbage trucks arrive at the transfer stations. How many garbage trucks will arrive at the transfer station within 6 hours?

6. The transfer station can process 350 tons of garbage a day. How many tons of garbage is that every 7 days?

# Day 78

Name: ____________________

Score:

**Facts:**

- **Gorillas are the largest primate.**
- **Males grow gray hair on their backs, which is why males are often called "silverbacks."**

1. On average, a silverback is twice as heavy as a female. If females weigh about 200 pounds, how heavy is the average silverback?

2. Adult gorillas eat about 50 pounds of food a day. Knowing this, how many pounds of food would you expect a group of 12 adults to eat?

3. A zoo feeds its adult gorillas 350 pounds of food a day. Knowing this, how many adult gorillas does the zoo likely have? *(Use the information from question 2.)*

**Facts:**

- **Gorillas are very strong. It's said that they can lift and throw 1,800 pounds of weight.**
- **They are usually gentle animals and are not considered aggressive but will defend their troop members if they feel threatened.**
- **Gorillas have opposable thumbs and a semi-opposable toe on each foot.**
- **Some captive gorillas have learned to communicate using sign language.**

4. If a gorilla knew 179 words in sign language when she was 3 years old and 243 more words by the time she was 5 years old, how many words did this gorilla know when she turned 5?

5. There were 83 gorillas living on a mountain range, but many died because of poachers and an outbreak of the Ebola virus. There are now only 59 gorillas left on the mountain range. How many fewer gorillas is that?

6. Gorillas live in groups called a troop. If one troop in the valley has 27 members, another troop has 16 members, and a third troop has 19 members, how many gorillas are there in the three troops combined?

**Trivia:**

- **What percent of DNA do gorillas and humans share?**

Name: ____________________

Score:

1. Charlie is a painter. If he sells 3 large paintings for £675 each and 5 small paintings for £350 each. how much money did Charlie make?

2. Charlie needs to buy a new set of paints that cost £95, brushes for £14, palettes for £25, canvas for £19, and linseed oil for £7. How much will he need to pay for these items?

3. There are a total of 5 halls designated for Charlie's painting exhibit. If one of them can only display 15 paintings and the rest can display 24 paintings each, how many paintings are there in Charlie's exhibit?

4. 128 guests came to view Charlie's exhibit the first hour it opened. During the next 4 hours, the exhibit only had an average of 54 guests per hour. How many guests did his exhibit have all together?

5. A guest from the exhibit wants Charlie to paint murals on the wall of her child's school. She offers Charlie £1,800 to paint the murals. Charlie thinks this job will take him 3 days to complete. If he accepts the offer, how much money will it be per day of work?

6. Charlie agreed to paint the mural. The wall that needs to be painted is 3 meters tall and 15 meters long. How many square meters does he need to paint?

Name: ______________________

Score:

**Facts:**

- **Oceans make up about 70% of the Earth's surface and may be the home of over 90% of Earth's life.**
- **96% of the water on the planet is in the oceans.**

(1) Roughly 2,000 new species are discovered in the oceans each year. How many new species is that each decade?

(2) Many experts believe that ocean plankton produces at least half of the oxygen on Earth. If there is 100 mL of oxygen in a person's breath of air, how much of that oxygen is probably produced by ocean plankton?

(3) Roger wants to sail a boat from California to Japan. If this journey is about 5,355 miles long and his sailboat travels about 105 miles a day, how long will it take him to complete this journey?

**Facts:**

- **The Pacific Ocean is the largest and deepest.**
- **"Pacific" means peaceful. (The Pacific Ocean was calm when Magellan named it in 1520.)**
- **The Mariana Trench is the deepest part of the ocean. More people have been to the moon than to the bottom of this trench.**

(4) The Mariana Trench is about 36,200 feet deep. Roughly how many miles deep is that? (*Hint: There are 5280 feet in a mile*. Round to the nearest mile)

(5) According to the United States Geological Survey, there are about 321,000,000 cubic miles of ocean water, but only about 22,339 cubic miles of surface freshwater (such as the water found in lakes and rivers) on earth. How much more ocean water is that than surface freshwater?

**Facts:**

- **The ocean floor is mostly unexplored.**
- **The surface of Mars has been better mapped than the ocean floor.**

(6) Every 1 kilogram of ocean water contains about 35 grams of salt. Knowing this, how many grams of salt would there be in 20 kilograms of ocean water?

**Trivia:**

- **If the oceans were empty, how long would it take the Amazon River to fill the oceans back up with water?**

# Day 81

Name: ______________________

Score:

1. Three groups of scuba divers will explore an underwater shipwreck. The first group is composed of 5 divers, the second group with 7 divers, and the last group with 4 divers. How many scuba divers are there in all?

2. The number of scuba divers exploring the shipwreck this year is 5 times as much as scuba divers last year. If 85 scuba divers went to the shipwreck last year, how many scuba divers went there this year?

3. Rex has been scuba diving for 7 years. If he is 31 years old now, how old was he when he started scuba diving?

4. The ship being explored is 428 feet long. If Rex can only swim 2 feet per second, how long will it take him to swim the entire length of the ship? *(Give your answer in minutes and seconds.)*

5. Coral has started to grow on the wrecked ship. One of the scuba divers shared that this coral grows at a rate of 3 millimeters per year. At this rate, how long would it take the coral to grow 4.5 centimeters tall?

6. The oxygen tank Rex is using holds 50 minutes of oxygen. But he wants to be safe and make it back to the surface with 10 minutes of oxygen left. If Rex has already been diving for 27 minutes, how much more time does he have before he should resurface?

# Day 82

Name: ______________________

Score:

**Facts:**

- **In many cultures, dragonflies symbolize good luck.**
- **Dragonflies are not known for biting humans. Their jaws are usually too weak to break the skin.**

(1) Fossils of dragonflies with 2-foot wingspans have been found. How many times wider is that than a modern-day dragonfly with a 4-inch wingspan?

(2) There are 40 dragonflies by a pond and they each catch about 115 bugs a day. How many bugs a day is that all together?

**Facts:**

- **Dragonflies cannot walk but are excellent fliers. They can fly forward, side-to-side, backward, and hover like a helicopter.**
- **Dragonflies are excellent hunters and can catch and eat hundreds of bugs each day.**

(3) If a dragonfly catches 78 bugs one day, 139 bugs the next day, and 124 bugs the day after that, how many bugs did it catch during those 3 days?

(4) If a dragonfly can fly 35 miles an hour, how far can it fly in 6 hours?

(5) Dragonflies begin their lives as nymphs and live underwater. If one dragonfly spends 2 years in its nymph form and then lives 2 months in its adult form, how many months long was its life?

(6) Fish love to eat dragonfly nymphs. If one trout ate 189 nymphs this week, on average, how many nymphs did this trout eat each day?

**Trivia:**

- **The globe skimmer is a dragonfly species that may have a longer migration route than any other insect. How many miles long is this migration route?**

Name: ____________________

Score:

① It's Sophia's birthday next week. She invited 13 friends from school, 5 cousins, and 8 neighbors to her birthday party. Out of all these people she invited, only 6 people were not able to attend the party. How many people did attend the party?

② Sophia's parents bought a container of vanilla ice-cream and a container of chocolate ice-cream. Each container contains 40 scoops of ice-cream. If 20 people want to eat ice-cream and her parents give each of these people an equal amount, how many scoops should each person get?

③ Sophia's mother booked 4 clowns to perform at the party. The fee for each clown costs £35 per hour. How much would she need to pay for all the clowns if they need to perform for a total of one and a half hours?

④ Mr. Cruz bought cupcakes for his daughter's birthday party that cost £1.27 each. How much did he pay if he purchased 45 cupcakes?

⑤ The 45 cupcakes Mr. Cruz bought came in equal amounts of 3 different flavors. How many cupcakes is that for each flavor?

⑥ They decided to play a game of volleyball at the party. If 26 people want to play volleyball and they want an equal amount of people on each of the two teams, how many people should be on each team?

# Day 84

**Facts:**

**- Roman soldiers often brought cherries on their conquests and spit the pits on the ground as they traveled, essentially planting countless cherry trees across the empire.**

Name: ____________________

Score:

1. Max and Peter went to a farm to get some fresh cherries. Max picked 246 in the morning, 312 in the afternoon, and 287 in the evening. Peter, on the other hand, picked 321 in the morning, 429 in the afternoon, and 312 in the evening. What is the total number of cherries they picked together?

2. Each cherry tree can produce about 7,000 cherries. If the farm needs a total of 294,000 cherries to supply all their customers, how many cherry trees will they need to harvest?

**Facts:**

**- Cherries are extremely nutritious and may help prevent heart disease and some forms of cancer.**

**- They are sometimes used to make perfume scents.**

3. A truck can carry a total of 45 boxes of cherries each trip. If each box weighs 15 kilograms, how many kilograms of cherries can the truck transport in 3 trips?

4. Last year, the farm harvested 3 tons of cherries per acre. This year, the farmers harvested 5 tons of cherries per acre. If the farm has 5 acres of cherry trees, how many more tons of cherries did the farm harvest this year than last year?

**Facts:**

**- Cherry trees can grow about 7,000 cherries each year and produce fruit for over a hundred years.**

5. The sour cherry tree is 20 feet shorter than the sweet cherry tree. If the sweet cherry tree is 36 feet tall, how tall is the sour cherry tree?

6. Hanna uses 3 pounds of cherries to make a large cherry pie and 1.5 pounds for a small sized cherry pie. If she wants to bake 15 large pies and 12 small sized cherry pies, how many pounds of cherries will she need?

**Trivia:**

**- What is a Staccato cherry?**

Name: ____________________

Score:

(1) Dan's dirt bike is 12 kg lighter than his motorcycle.
If his motorcycle is 93 kg, how heavy is his dirt bike?

(2) Several riders are competing in a dirt bike race in Arizona. The fee for joining the race is £320. How much money was collected if 27 riders are joining the event?

(3) Dan finished the race in second place with a time of 42 minutes and 35 seconds.
The first place winner finished 2 minutes and 40 seconds earlier than Dan.
How long did it take the first place winner to finish the race?

(4) The third place winner received £1250, the second place winner received £2,500, and the first place winner received £5,000. How much prize money is that total?

(5) 194 adults and 83 children watched the dirt bike race. If adult entrance tickets cost £7 each and children's entrance tickets cost £4 each, how much money was collected from the entrance ticket sales?

(6) Dan was hungry after the race. He ordered 2 hamburgers for £5.25 each, a soda for £1.75, and a bag of chips for £2.00. If he pays for these items with a 20-pound note, how much change should he receive?

Name: ____________________

Score:

**Facts:**

- **Hedgehogs received their name because they are often found near bushes and hedges and because they make grunting noises like pigs.**

1. If one hedgehog has 5,628 spines and a larger hedgehog has 6,305 spines, how many more spines does the larger hedgehog have?

2. If a hedgehog gave birth 7 times during its life and each time it birthed 6 piglets, how many piglets did it birth altogether?

**Facts:**

- **Hedgehogs can have as many as 7,000 spines.**
- **The spines lay flat when the hedgehog is calm.**
- **When scared, the spines will stick up and the hedgehog will curl into a ball for protection.**

3. If a pet store sold 74 hedgehogs one year and 92 hedgehogs the next year, how many hedgehogs were sold altogether?

4. Lilly's hedgehog weighed 218 grams when she bought it from the pet store. 4 weeks later, it weighed 350 grams. On average, how much weight did it gain each week?

5. If Lilly feeds her hedgehog 30 cat kibbles each day, how many cat kibbles will it eat in 3 weeks?

6. Hedgehogs are nocturnal and very active at night. They often run 3 km each night. At this rate, how many nights would it take a hedgehog to run 75 km?

**Trivia:**

- **What is a group of hedgehogs called?**

Name: ____________________

Score:

① Amy works as a babysitter. She earns £11 per hour.
If she worked for a total of 42 hours last month, how much did she earn?

② Amy wants to buy a new phone that costs £528. If she is saving £88 per week, how long will it take her to save enough money to buy the phone?

③ When Amy finally went to buy the phone, she learned that it was on sale.
If the phone was normally priced at £528 but Amy received it for £459, how much money did the sale save her?

④ Amy found a new family to babysit for. They have 3 children and want to pay her £4.50 per hour per child. If she earned 54 pounds the first evening she babysat them, how many hours did she work?

⑤ Amy is making spaghetti and meat balls for the 3 children. If she has 21 meatballs and wants to give an equal amount to each of the children, how many meatballs should each child get?

⑥ Amy is also slicing apples to feed the 3 children, but Amy wants to eat some of the apples too. If she gives everyone, including herself 8 apple slices, how many apple slices did they have all together?

# Day 88

Name: ____________________

Score:

**Facts:**

- **The telescope was patented in 1608 by Hans Lippershey.**
- **Hans' telescope could magnify objects 3 times (3x).**

① William Herschel was the first person to discover Uranus. He used a 7-foot-long telescope to see it. He wanted to view things better, so he later built a 40-foot telescope. How much longer was his 40-foot telescope than the first telescope he saw Uranus with?

② If Hershel's giant telescope had a magnification of 6,450x, how many times stronger was this magnification than the telescope Hans Lippershey first patented?

**Facts:**

- **Galileo Galilei was the first scientist to use the telescope to study objects in outer space.**
- **He learned to make his own telescopes. By 1609, he had made one with a 20x magnification.**
- **Galileo used his studies to prove that the Earth revolves around the sun. Back then, most people thought the sun revolved around the Earth.**
- **He also discovered that Saturn had rings, Jupiter had moons, and that the Milky Way was a massive group of individual stars.**

③ A laboratory's telescope had its objective lens replaced every 3 years and its eyepiece replaced every 4 years since it was built 108 years ago. How many times has the eyepiece been replaced?

④ The laboratory built a new telescope. It can view objects that are 11 million light years further away than the old telescope could view. If the old telescope could view objects 2 million light years away, what are the furthest objects the new telescope can view?

**Aperture** is the diameter of the opening that allows light into a telescope or camera.

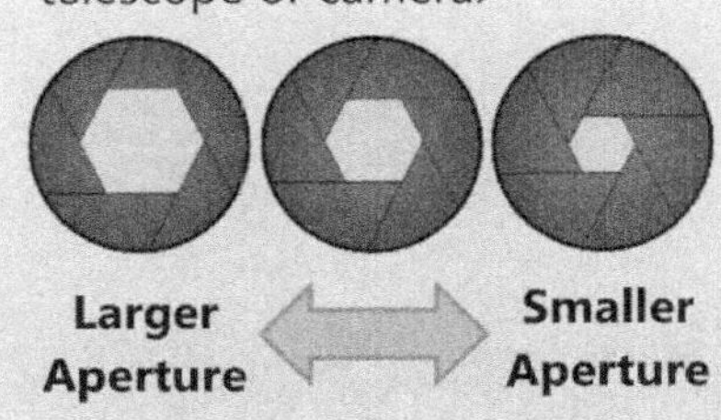


⑤ Kelly's old telescope had an aperture of 80mm. Her new telescope has an aperture size that is 25mm larger than her old telescope. What is the aperture of Kelly's new telescope?

⑥ Adam needs to buy 8 new telescopes for his team.
If each telescope costs £450, how much money will he need to purchase them all?

**Trivia:**

- **Why was Galileo placed under house arrest for the rest of his life?**

Name: ____________________

Score:

① Chef Lee is preparing food for his customers and has a budget of £450. He bought carrots for £89, potatoes for £75, cabbage for £50, onions for £45, and meat for £167. How much money is left on Chef Lee's budget?

② Chef Lee wants to boil the meat for 40 minutes. If he started boiling the meat at 9:53 AM, what time should the meat be done boiling?

③ Chef Lee can peel 8 potatoes every 5 minutes. If he has 360 potatoes to peel, how many minutes should Chef Lee expect to spend peeling potatoes?

④ Chef Lee normally sells a steak dinner for £18 each, but agreed to sell 80 steak dinners to a customer for £1,280. How much money is that for each steak dinner?

⑤ Chef Lee has 7 servers working in his restaurant tonight. If each server can serve 16 customers at a time, how many customers can the restaurant serve at a time tonight?

⑥ The restaurant had 500 to-go boxes at the start of the week, but now they only have 48 left. How many to-go boxes did the restaurant use this week?

# Day 90

Name: ____________________

Score:

## Facts:

- Giant tortoises can weigh over 500 pounds.
- The smallest tortoise species has an adult shell length that is less than 4 inches long.

1. Aldabra tortoises often have shells that are 48 inches long. How many times longer is that than the shell of the smallest tortoise species?
*(Use the information from the Facts box.)*

2. If a tortoise walks at a speed of 352 feet an hour, how long would it take the tortoise to travel a mile?
*(Hint: There are 5280 feet in a mile.)*

## Facts:

- Tortoises only live on land and are not suited for living in water.
- Tortoises often live to be 100 and sometimes close to 200 years old.
- Tortoises mostly eat plants. A few species will occasionally eat meat.
- Their shells have nerves that can sense when things touch the shell.

3. A 15-year-old tortoise weighed 42 pounds. When this same tortoise was 35 years old it weighed 82 pounds. On average, how many pounds did this tortoise gain each year?

4. There were 14,000 tortoises on an island. Then, sailors discovered the island and began capturing the tortoises for food. 60 years later, there were only 582 tortoises left on the island. How many fewer tortoises is that?

## Facts:

- Sailors used to love eating tortoises.
- Tortoises were easy to capture and survived well on ships, providing fresh meat during the months at sea.

5. One of the captured tortoises was not eaten, but given to the Queen as a gift. If this tortoise was 46 years old when it was captured and lived another 117 years, how old was this tortoise when it died?

6. A tortoise at the zoo eats 5 apples and 2 oranges each day. How many items of fruit is that each week?

## Trivia:

- How old is the oldest tortoise?

Name: ____________________

Score:

1. An automobile factory can manufacture 4,750 tires per day.
If the factory operates 6 days a week, how many tires does it manufacture a week?

2. Edward does the engine installation for the automobile factory. He can place an engine in a new automobile in 4 minutes. At this rate, how many engines can he place in an hour?

3. The goal of the production team of the company is to manufacture 4,600 automobiles a month. If there are about 4 weeks in a month, how many automobiles will they need to make a week to meet their monthly goal?

4. The automobile factory has 2,754 employees. If 1,652 of the employees work on the assembly line, 796 employees work in the service center, and the rest work in the administration department, how many employees work in the administration department?

5. The company uses a total of 64 metal sheets to create a four-seater car.
How many four-seater cars can be made using 24,700 metal sheets?

6. The automobile company earns £17,950,000 each month but needs to use some of this money to pay its employees. If the 2,754 employees are paid an average of £3,500 each per month, how much money does the company make a month after paying its employees?

**Facts:**

- **The Earth is believed to be about 4.5 billion years old.**
- **It takes Earth 365 days, 5 hours, 59 minutes and 16 seconds to orbit the sun.**

Name: ____________________

Score:

1. Earth's atmosphere is about 78% nitrogen, 21% oxygen and the rest is made of "trace gasses," such as argon and carbon dioxide. What percentage of the atmosphere is made of trace gasses?

2. About 71% of Earth's surface is covered with water. The rest is covered with land. What percentage of Earth's surface is land?

**Facts:**

- **Earth might look round, but it's not a perfect sphere. Its rotation causes it to bulge a little at the equator.**
- **Its shape is more like a squished ball. This shape is called an oblate sphere.**

3. Earth's equator has a circumference of about 24,901 miles, while the circumference passing through the poles is about 24,860 miles. How much larger is the circumference at the equator than the poles?

4. Earth travels through space at a speed of about 67,000 miles per hour. At this rate, how many hours would it take to travel 335,000 miles?

5. If Earth travels through space at a speed of about 67,000 miles per hour, how far would it travel in a day?

**Facts:**

- **Earth is the 3rd planet from the sun and the 5th largest planet in the solar system.**

6. The oldest rocks ever found on earth are believed to be 4.28 billion years old. If Earth is estimated to be 4.5 billion years old, how old was Earth when these rocks formed?

**Trivia:**

- **Where were the oldest rocks on earth found?**

Name: ____________________

Score:

1. An auto repair shop has a total of 12 mechanics, 15 technicians, and 8 clerks.
How many employees is that?

2. An average automotive technician replaces a tire in 8 minutes and 10 seconds.
If Larry can do the same job in 6 minutes and 35 seconds,
how much faster is he than an average automotive technician?

3. Michael wanted to replace all the tires in the pre-owned SUV he bought. If he wants an all-terrain tire that costs £115 per tire, how much does he need to pay for a set of 4 tires?

4. Jake is a car racer. If he schedules his car maintenance for every 2 months,
how many maintenance appointments is that per year?

5. The shop is celebrating its anniversary. So they will be giving a £5 discount for every £50 repair cost. Jim has his brakes fixed for £376. How much of a discount will he receive?

6. Amy needs to have her car's brake, battery, and oil replaced. The shop inspector quoted that the cost for brake replacement is £85, battery replacement is £195, and changing of oil is £32. How much is that for all the repairs?

# Day 94

Name: ____________________

Score:

**Facts:**

**- A cubic millimeter of blood has about 4–5 million red blood cells and about 5,000–10,000 white blood cells.**

① If an adult human heart pumps 1,800 gallons of blood each day, how many gallons of blood would it pump each week?

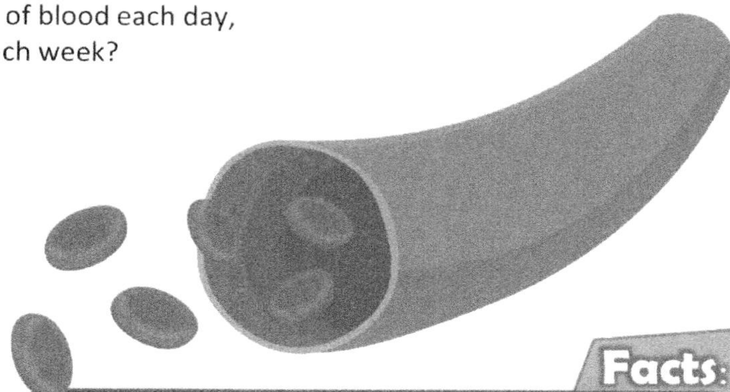

② A red blood cell can live for about 120 days. How many months is that?
*(Estimate that there are 30 days in a month.)*

**Facts:**

- **Red blood cells bring oxygen to your body.**
- **White blood cells fight diseases and infections.**
- **New blood cells are made in your bone marrow.**
- **An adult body contains about 11 pints of blood.**

③ If a cubic millimeter of a person's blood has 5 million red blood cells and 5,000 white blood cells, how many times more red blood cells are there than white blood cells?

④ Donating 1 pint of blood may save the lives of 3 people. If Crystal has donated 16 pints in her lifetime, how many lives could her donations have saved?

⑤ The blood drive had 2,561 people donate blood the first day of the drive and 2,794 people donate blood the second day of the drive. How many people donated blood all together?

⑥ Leo went to the drive to donate blood for the first time. He arrived at 9:27 AM and finished donating at 9:51 AM. How long did it take him to donate his blood?

**Trivia:**

**- How much gold is in your blood?**

Name: ____________________

Score:

(1) The art museum is in an eight-story building that displays paintings from different eras. If each floor displays 87 paintings, how many paintings are there in the art museum?

(2) 278 adults and 103 kids visited the museum yesterday. Today, 345 adults and 216 kids visited the museum. How many more people visited the museum today than yesterday?

(3) A school went to the art museum for a field trip. The museum usually charges £12 for each child but agreed to give the school a £5 discount for each student. How many students did the school bring to the museum if it paid £1,253 to the museum for its students to enter?

(4) It was reported that there was a total of 4,436 visitors in May, 5,328 visitors in June, 5,094 visitors in July, and 4,925 visitors in August. How many visitors visited the museum in these 4 months?

(5) Reya's family is visiting the museum. They need to buy 3 adult tickets for £15 and 4 children's tickets for £12. How much money is that for her family?

(6) The museum purchases a set of 6 paintings for a new exhibit. If it paid an average of £4,600 for each of these paintings, how much is that for the whole set?

Name: ____________________

Score:

**Facts:**

- **Most skydivers jump from an altitude of 14,000 feet.**
- **People have survived higher falls than this without a parachute. It's rare, but things like tree branches or thick snow can slow a person enough to survive.**

1. A skydiver freefalls at a speed of about 120 miles per hour when their stomach is facing Earth but can fall 180 miles per hour if they fall headfirst with their feet up. How much faster can a person fall when positioned headfirst?

2. A parachute slows a person's fall to about 12 miles per hour. How many times slower is that than a 180 mile per hour freefall?

**Facts:**

- **An altimeter is a tool used to measure altitude.**
- **Skydivers often wear an altimeter on their wrist, like a watch, so they know how high they are and when it's time to deploy their parachute.**

3. Skydivers often deploy their parachute at 5,000 feet above the ground. After that, it takes about 5 minutes to reach the ground. Roughly how many feet per minute do they fall once the parachute is deployed?

**Facts:**

- **André-Jacques Garnerin invented the parachute and performed the first parachute jump in 1797.**
- **That's over 100 years before airplanes existed.**
- **A hydrogen balloon lifted him 3,200 feet above Paris for the first test jump. Thankfully, it worked.**

4. Rosie and 2 of her friends will skydive to celebrate her 26th birthday. If it costs £240 for each person to jump, how much will it cost for all 3 of them combined?

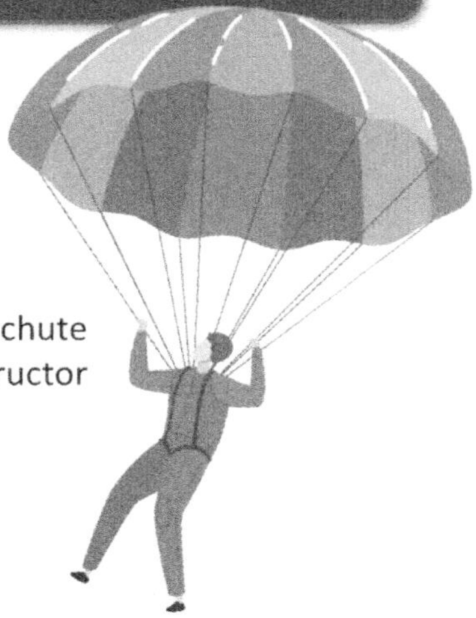

5. This is Rosie's first skydive, so she will be attached to an instructor. Their parachute can hold up to 450 pounds of weight. If Rosie weighs 155 pounds and her instructor weighs 187 pounds, how much more weight could their parachute hold.

6. Cody's altimeter was damaged during his last parachute jump. When buying a new altimeter, he gave the store clerk four 20-pound notes. If the cost of the altimeter is £65.99, how much change should Cody receive?

**Trivia:**

- **How high was the highest parachute jump?**

Name: ____________________

Score:

① A cruise ship is sailing in Antarctica carrying passengers of which 245 are adults and 89 are kids. If there are also 89 employees on the ship, what is the total number of people on the ship?

② The average passenger cruise expense per day is £275 of which £148 is for the ticket price and the rest is for board spending. How much money a day does the average passenger use for board spending?

③ The speed of the cruise ship is 23 miles per hour. How many days will the cruise last if the ship will be travelling a total of 2,760 miles?

④ A family composed of 4 adults and 3 kids are cruising across the Southern Ocean. If each of their tickets for the cruise was £740, what was the total cost of this family's tickets?

⑤ The family had an option to pay an extra £159 to become first class passengers. If there are 7 people in the family, how much more would they need to pay to all become first class passengers?

⑥ The length of the cruise ship is six times its width. If the width measures 127 feet, what is the length of the ship?

# Day 98

Name: ____________________

Score:

**Facts:**

- **Tarantulas are some of the largest spiders on Earth.**
- **Tarantulas molt as they grow, meaning they will grow new exoskeletons and shed their old ones.**

1. Tarantulas dig burrows using their fangs. If one tarantula is digging with a speed of 4 centimeters per minute, how long would it take the tarantula to dig 3 burrows with a length of 52 centimeters each?

2. A tarantula laid 957 eggs but only 882 of them hatched. How many eggs did not hatch?

**Facts:**

- **Tarantulas are cold-blooded.**
- **They love to eat crickets, worms, beetles, and grasshoppers. Larger Tarantulas will eat mice, birds, frogs, and lizards too.**
- **A tarantula can lay 2,000 eggs at a time.**
- **Nearly 1,000 species have been identified.**

3. The pet store keeps 8 tarantulas in each tank. How many tarantula tanks are there in the pet store if they have a total of 136 tarantulas?

4. Randy bought a pet tarantula when he was 9 years old. The pet store owner told him at the time that his tarantula could live another 25 years. How old would Randy be at that time?

5. Randy bought 45 crickets and 36 silkworms for his pet tarantula. If he paid £0.40 for every 5 crickets and £1.29 for every dozen silkworms, how much money did he spend?

6. There were already 7 crickets in his tarantula's tank before Randy dropped in 10 more crickets and 5 silkworms. By the end of the day, his tarantula ate 4 of the crickets. How many crickets are left in the tank?

**Trivia:**

- **What is the largest species of tarantula?**

Name: ____________________

Score:

① An animal shelter in Springfield has 81 dogs, 35 cats, 12 guinea pigs, 8 rabbits, and 16 hamsters. How many animals in total are there in the shelter?

② How many more dogs are there than cats, guinea pigs, rabbits, and hamsters combined? *(Use the information from question 1.)*

③ The dogs in the shelter can consume 2 sacks of food per week. How many sacks of dog food can be consumed in a month?

④ Jeff takes the dogs for a walk each day. If he brings 3 dogs with him for each walk, how many walks would he need to take to walk all 81 dogs at the shelter?

⑤ The animal shelter received £749 of donations in August and £785 of donations in September. How much money was donated in August and September combined?

⑥ The animal shelter's goal is to receive a total of £9,000 of donations by the end of the year. If the animal shelter has already received £6,516 and has 3 more months before the end of the year, on average, how much more money would the animal shelter need to receive each month to meet its goal?

# Day 100

Name: ____________________

Score:

**Facts:**

- **Jellyfish are not fish, which is why many people prefer to simply call them "Jellies."**
- **Jellies do not have a brain, heart, or bones.**
- **Many species glow in the dark.**

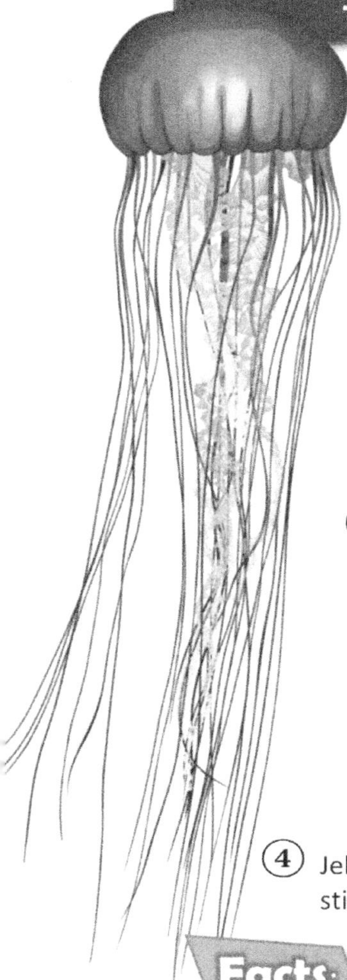

1. A group of jellies is often called a "bloom." One bloom had 430,020 jellies in it, until a school of tuna ate 28,683 of the jellies. How many jellies are left in the bloom now?

2. The largest known species is the lion's mane jellyfish. They can be 120 feet long. How many times longer is that than the length of a 30-foot school bus?

**Facts:**

- **Jellies produce venomous toxins but only some species create toxins that are harmful to humans.**
- **These toxins often help the jellies to capture their prey, by paralyzing fish that touch their tentacles.**
- **The Australian box jellyfish is believed to be the most poisonous creature in the ocean. A box jellyfish sting can kill a person in a few minutes.**

3. The lion's mane jellyfish can grow to weigh 200 pounds. If Tyler weighs 83 pounds, how much heavier is a 200-pound lion's mane jellyfish?

4. Jellyfish tentacles have stinging cells called cnidocytes. Cnidocytes have a tiny needle-like stinger that injects venom into things that touch them. If 1,462,874 cnidocytes stung Abby's left leg and 604,287 stung her right leg, how many cnidocytes stung her all together?

**Facts:**

- **Many jellyfish species are edible.**
- **They're usually salty, slimy, and chewy.**

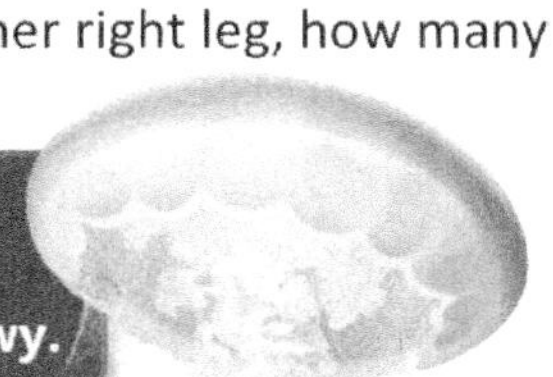

5. Abby was stung by the jellyfish at 10:47 in the morning and arrived at the hospital at 11:04 AM. How long did it take her to get to the hospital after getting stung?

6. A doctor wants Abby to receive 6 mg of antivenom. If 1 mL of antivenom medication contains 3 mg of antivenom, how many mL of the medication should the nurse give Abby?

**Trivia:**

- **How small is the smallest jellyfish species?**

# Answers

## Day 1:
1) 35 meters
2) 6,960 silver coins
3) 343 silver coins
4) 140 stones
5) 192 bags of cement
6) 1,791 meals

## Day 2:
1) 4 times hotter
2) 731 million volts
3) 90 people
4) Speed of light
5) 3 miles
6) 100 times
Trivia) Fulminology is the study of lightning. Would you like to become a fulminologist?

## Day 3:
1) 5 times more
2) 13 fish
3) 56 worms
4) 34 bluegills
5) 5 pounds 13 ounces
6) 33 pounds

## Day 4:
1) 9,268 km wider
2) three hundred eighty-four thousand, four hundred km.
3) 21 days
4) 255 **°C cooler**
5) 366 **°C** colder
6) 240 grams
Trivia) About 2.5 seconds.

## Day 5:
1) £22
2) 1:45 PM
3) 120 minutes (2hours)
4) 75 pounds
5) £50
6) £60.72

## Day 6:
1) AA battery
2) 4 times longer
3) 10.5 mm
4) 560 times
5) 156 flowers
6) 20 hours
Trivia) Some hummingbird hearts can beat over 1,200 times a minute. (Over 20 beats per second!)

## Day 7:
1) £98
2) 8 packs
3) 20 pounds
4) 2,100 people
5) 21 feet
6) 52 feet

## Day 8:
1) 68 cm
2) 108 kg
3) 502.3 million ounces of gold
4) 100.5 million ounces of gold
5) 19 gold nuggets
6) Each treasure hunter gets 356 gold coins and they donate 2 gold coins.
Trivia): See the next column →

## Day 8: *Continued*
Trivia) Gold is soft. Miners used to test nuggets by biting them. If teeth marks were left in the nugget, they knew it was gold and high purity nuggets were easier to bite into than low purity nuggets. Traders used to check the purity of gold coins by biting them too.

In modern times, Olympic champions are often seen biting their gold medals too. They usually aren't testing the purity of their gold. It's just something fun to do in front of the cameras.

Your dentist probably wouldn't recommend biting nuggets, coins, or medals though, so bite carefully. Better yet, just don't bite them at all.

## Day 9:
1) 4 times more
2) 5,879 fiction books
3) 19 days
4) 39 books
5) 750 books
6) 5 hours and 44 minutes (344 minutes)

## Day 10:
11) 18 years
2) 6 pounds of chocolate
3) 300 cacao beans
4) 72 gold coins
5) 131 million pounds
6) No. There would be 70 (35 x 2) insect fragments in 100 grams, which is above the limit.
Trivia) Dark chocolate is mostly made of cocoa and cocoa butter. It does not have milk or milk butter in it like milk chocolate does. 50% or more of a dark chocolate bar is usually made from cocoa, while milk chocolate may only contain 10% cocoa.

Dark chocolate usually doesn't have as much added sugars as milk chocolates do either. Most experts agree that eating modest amounts of dark chocolate is healthier than eating milk chocolates.

## Day 11:
1) £529
2) £78
3) 962 toothbrushes
4) 8 procedures
5) £9,405
6) £1,120 each day

## Day 12:
1) 2 hour and 16 minutes
2) 270 eggs
3) 63 hatchlings
4) 9 hatchlings
5) 10 200-pound men
6) 48 transmitters
Trivia) Sharks and killer whales will try to bite the flippers off sea turtles, but other predators are rare. Humans are by far the most dangerous for sea turtles. Turtle hunting and the collecting of eggs have decimated sea turtle populations over the centuries.

## Day 13:
1) £26.40 (Peter is buying fuel for <u>both</u> of them.)
2) 2,449 tickets
3) 19 racecars
4) 177 miles
5) 86 miles
6) £5,000

## Day 14:
1) 1,125 grams
2) 11,469 synapses
3) 115,804,366,057,295
4) 17% more oxygen
5) 400 calories
6) 137 milligrams
Trivia) Many seafoods, such as sardines, salmon, oysters, and shrimp have high levels of omega-3 fatty acids. Walnuts, flax seeds, and brussels sprouts are other examples of foods that contain omega-3 fatty acids.

## Day 15:
1) 636 buckets of dirt
2) 48 dinosaur bones per day
3) 56 cm longer
4) 54 bones
5) 29 bones
6) 76.2 million years older

## Day 16:
1) 32 magnets
2) 12 poles
3) 13 tons more
4) 175 miles per hour faster
5) 4 hours
6) 26 minutes
Trivia) No, a cow magnet does not attract cows. A cow magnet is like a large magnetic pill that some farmers make their cows swallow.

This may sound mean, but it could save the cow's life. A cow magnet remains inside the cow the rest of its life and collects pieces of metal the cow accidentally eats, such as nails, fencing, or other metal fragments. It can prevent these metal pieces from passing through the digestive system, potentially saving the cow from serious injuries.

## Day 17:
1) 250 news reports
2) 27 men
3) £40,200
4) 28 reports
5) 5 times longer
6) 5 reports each hour

## Day 18:
1) 3,000 eggs
2) 18 hours
3) 27 days
4) 417 did not survive
5) 50 seconds
6) 17 flies
Trivia) Yes, house flies can't eat solid foods, so they turn solid foods into a liquid first. They vomit digestive fluids onto the food. These juices liquify the solids so the fly can drink it.

Basically, house flies can't wait to land on your food, so they can vomit, drink, and probably poop while they're there.

## Day 19:
1) 17 mail sorters
2) 5,400,000 pieces of mail
3) 7,200 pieces of mail
4) 4,800 pieces of mail
5) 3,154 envelopes
6) £10.55

# Answers

## Day 20:

1) 128 liters of popcorn
2) 158 **°C**
3) 5 pounds and 57 cents profit
4) 192,000 bags
5) 300 grams
6) 15 million more pounds

Trivia) Butterfly popcorn (top photo) has "wings" after it's popped. The wings take up space, giving butterfly popcorn an airy, fluffy look. Taking up space also is great for movie theaters because they don't have to pop as many kernels to fill a bag. That means more profits for the theaters.

Butterfly popcorn is usually soft, making it easier for people to chew too. The wings on butterfly popcorn are also good for catching seasonings, such as butter and salt.

Mushroom popcorn (lower photo) is round when it's popped and stronger than popped butterfly popcorn. These qualities make them better suited for making candy popcorn, such as caramel or chocolate covered popcorns. The soft wings of butterfly popcorn would break under the weight.

## Day 21:

1) 210 thunderstorms
2) 20,000 metric tons of rainfall
3) 60 miles per hour
4) 7,581 homes
5) 51 houses
6) £450 per pole

## Day 22:

1) 240 seconds
2) 9 eggshells
3) 2,290,372 bacteria
4) 4 years old
5) 0.55 grams more
6) 228 days

Trivia) Urine is a natural source of ammonia, which is an excellent cleaning chemical. That's why ancient Romans often added urine to their toothpaste. (They used urine to help wash their clothes too.) Urine remained a common ingredient in toothpastes until the 1800's.

## Day 23:

1) 105 minutes (1 hour and 45 Minutes)
2) 20 minutes
3) 16 minutes faster
4) 42 violation tickets
5) £4,975
6) £245

## Day 24:

1) 175 more times
2) 14,400 beats
3) 83 beats per minute
4) 121 beats per minute
5) 15 heart beats
6) 3:25 PM

Trivia) It depends how long a person lives and how many beats per minute their heart averages throughout their lifetime, but if there are 525,600 minutes in a year and a person's heart beats about 80 times a minute, then their heart would beat 42,048,000 times a year. If a person's heart beats that many times a year and they live to be 100, their heart would have beat over 4 billion times in their lifetime.



## Day 25:

1) 5,600 cookies
2) 840 cookies
3) 180 minutes (3 hours)
4) 10 slices
5) 1,200 cupcakes
6) £6,840

## Day 26:

1) 500 pounds heavier
2) 35 feet long
3) 6 times more fish
4) 24 minutes
5) 48 squid per whale
6) 7 more inches

Trivia) The southern pygmy squid is the smallest known squid species. Males grow less than 2 cm long, which is less than 1 inch.

## Day 27:

1) 840 beds
2) 19 rooms
3) 69 assistants
4) 18 patients
5) 5 hours
6) 115 boxes of gloves

## Day 28:

1) 75 grams of silver
2) 6 more meters
3) 3 more days
4) 1,641 more sticks
5) 1,560 cinnamon sticks
6) 6 grams of cinnamon powder

Trivia) Cinnamon trees are native to Sri Lanka and nearby coasts of India and Myanmar. Today cinnamon is grown in many different places and in different varieties. Some people refer to ceylon cinnamon, grown in Sri Lanka, to be "true cinnamon". Although Sri Lanka is still a huge cinnamon producer, most of the world's supply of cinnamon is a variety called cassia cinnamon, and most cassia cinnamon is grown in China and Indonesia. Chances are, if you have cinnamon in your kitchen cupboard, it's cassia cinnamon.

## Day 29:

1) 820 chickens per barn
2) 820,000 eggs
3) 2,735 chickens left
4) 25 sacks of feed
5) 15 days
6) £112,200

## Day 30:

1) 31 cm taller
2) 45 kg heavier
3) 3 12-kg packs
4) £400
5) 32 kg of fur
6) £570

Trivia) Alpaca hair is hollow which traps air and warmth. Hollow hairs also make their fleece lightweight. Despite being hollow, alpaca fleece is stronger than sheep wool. If that isn't impressive enough, alpaca fur is also more fire resistant than most other clothing fibers, it wicks away moisture, and is less likely to wrinkle than cashmere.

## Day 31:

1) 1,831,676 barrels of oil
2) £184,000,000
3) £78,000
4) 13 km per hour
5) 7,200 km
6) 80,000 barrels per hour

## Day 32:

1) 27 more berries
2) 4,423 seeds
3) 1,347 seeds
4) 25 months
5) 84,000 plants
6) 14 pounds

Trivia) Costa Rica may not be a large country, but when this book was created, Costa Rica was growing more pineapples than any other nation. The Philippines and Brazil are also top producers.

## Day 33:

1) 48 years old
2) £275
3) 12 feet of pipes
4) $135
5) 4 and a half hours
6) 1,095 gallons a year

## Day 34:

1) 16 times faster
2) 400 **°C**
3) 166 km wider
4) 30 meteors per minute
5) 600 meteors
6) £332,200

Trivia) Some lucky people see a meteorite fall nearby, and they find the place where it landed. That doesn't happen often. So, many people use metal detectors to search the ground for old meteorites. Many meteorites contain a lot of iron, which helps detectors to find them underground.

## Day 35:

1) £7
2) £19
3) 1,216 points
4) 795 points
5) 2,767 points
6) 1 and a half hours

## Day 36:

1) 32 times taller
2) 5 hours
3) 20 times slower
4) 1 hour and 23 minutes
5) 1,000 times longer
6) 5 severe tsunamis

Critical Thinking) It's wide wavelength and short height make it appear flat.

Trivia) People who live near the ocean often prepare for tsunamis the same way people prepare for fires or tornadoes. They make a safety plan and try identifying safe places to go during a tsunami.

Many countries try to detect tsunamis before they reach shore. This allows them to warn people of danger before the tsunami reaches land. Sensors on ocean buoys can detect tsunamis while they're still in the deep ocean. Any time an earthquake is detected, alert systems try to warn people near the ocean that a tsunami may occur.

During a tsunami warning, people near the ocean should try to quickly get to high ground. That's where a safety plan comes in handy. Knowing which places are the safest to go to and the fastest routes to get there could be the difference between life and death.

## Day 37:

1) 1,277 guests
2) 200 person seating capacity
3) 21 servers
4) £19
5) £70.05
6) 264 plates

## Day 38:
1) 210 more kg of salt
2) 700 grams of salt
3) 3,310 kg of salt
4) 6 grams of salt each
5) 14 °C lower
6) 2,648 tons of salt left over
Trivia) It depends on the person, so you should consult your doctor to find what the recommended amount of salt for you is. For most adults, anything more than 5 grams of salt a day is probably too much. (The pile of salt in the photograph is about 5 grams of salt.) It's important to remember that salt is already found in a lot of foods. Even when people don't sprinkle additional salt on their foods, they often eat over 5 grams of salt a day.

## Day 39:
1) £175,000
2) 1,642 tickets
3) £35 per airing
4) 3 hours and 45 minutes (225 minutes)
5) £20
6) £56

## Day 40:
1) 335,000 kg
2) 1,107,000 kg
3) 3 blue whales
4) 1,300 meters tall
5) 11 times larger
6) 80 °C colder
Trivia) Fog

## Day 41:
1) £185,084 per carat
2) 4 hours and 43 minutes
3) 7 minutes
4) 20 munites
5) 38 minutes
6) £405,000

## Day 42:
1) 0.7 million more visitors
2) 4.9 million kilowatts
3) 4,400 people
4) 3,300 feet of crest line
5) 3,045 feet taller
6) 320 feet wider
Trivia) It used to erode over 3 feet a year. Now that some water is diverted from the falls and steps are taken to reduce erosion, the rate has slowed. In recent years, Niagara Falls usually erodes less than a foot each year.

## Day 43:
1) 51 years old
2) 46 minor operations
3) 45 minutes longer
4) 180 milliliters of blood
5) 40 seconds
6) 2 hours and 55 minutes (175 minutes)

## Day 44:
1) 1,200 feet
2) 12,020 feet long
3) 3 hours and 40 minutes (220 minutes)
4) 117,539 passengers
5) 21 miles longer
6) 5.5 feet wider
Trivia) Badgers, gophers, and rabbits are great tunnel diggers, but Zambian mole rats take it to the next level. A colony of these mole rats can dig tunnel systems over a mile and a half long.

## Day 45:
1) 10 laps
2) 3,300,000 gallons of water
3) £86.94
4) 12 minutes and 40 seconds (760 seconds)
5) £17 more
6) 43 seconds

## Day 46:
1) 55 miles
2) 510 pounds
3) 35 pounds heavier
4) 5 times more calories
5) 23 miles longer
6) 5 hours and 53 minutes faster
Trivia) That person is called a "musher." They ride on the sled, behind the team, and often shout commands to the dogs. "Gee" is the command to turn right. "Haw" tells the dogs to turn left. "Mush" can roughly be translated to "let's go."

## Day 47:
1) £941
2) 128 apps
3) 17 minutes and 30 seconds long
4) 822MB
5) 12 minutes
6) 83 MB of RAM

## Day 48:
1) 4 carats
2) 1400 milligrams
3) 109 diamonds
4) 7 hours and 19 minutes
5) £959
6) 2,576 carats lighter
Trivia) The largest diamond ever found was named the Cullinan Diamond. It was found In South Africa and given to Britain's King Edward VII.

The largest piece cut from this diamond is named Cullinan I (AKA "the Great Star of Africa"). It is the world's largest colorless cut diamond.

Cullinan I was mounted in the Sovereign's Scepter with Cross, which is held by English royalty during their crowning ceremony.

The second largest cut piece from the Cullinan diamond was named Cullinan II. It was mounted to the front of the Imperial State Crown.

## Day 49:
1) 250 roses
2) 15 meters
3) 65 seeds
4) 684 flowers (57 flower dozens)
5) 560 grams of fertilizer
6) 20 wheelbarrow loads

## Day 50:
1) 8 minutes and 19 seconds
2) 262 seconds longer
3) 14,994,000 °C hotter
4) 13,020 km a minute
5) 9.6 billion years
6) 1.59 light years
Trivia) There are 3 stars in the Alpha Centauri solar system. Earth's solar system only has one star. Most solar systems have 2 or more stars. How odd would it be to look in the sky and see 2 or 3 suns?

## Day 51:
1) 4,726 buildings
2) £105,350
3) £92 per window
4) 11,567 homes
5) £1,212.50
6) £140,000

## Day 52:
1) 90 million salmon
2) 5,901 eggs
3) 78 salmon
4) 52,517 salmon
5) 9 salmon per minute
6) 11:12 AM
Trivia) A large, upstream migration of salmon is called a "salmon run." Sometimes, it can be hard to see the bottom of a river because there are so many salmon swimming by.

## Day 53:
1) 23 years old
2) 159 pounds
3) 80 shirts
4) 42 pounds
5) 60 mL of oil
6) 17 and a half hours (17.5 hours)

## Day 54:
1) 1911
2) 41 km per hour faster
3) 14 years
4) 9 °C colder
5) 16,105 more tourists
6) 27,200 people
Trivia) Male emperor penguins remain inland to keep eggs warm while females live by the ocean for weeks to hunt and feed.

## Day 55:
1) 84 feet taller
2) 167 days
3) 24 gallons
4) 140 lighthouses
5) £2,107
6) 15 years

## Day 56:
1) 160 gallons of sap
2) 135 gallons of sap
3) 80 pounds
4) 12 hours
5) 600 pounds
6) £2,680
Trivia) Fake maple syrup? Yes, most "maple syrups" sold at grocery stores are either fake or they only have very small amounts of actual maple syrup in them. Most of these products use corn starch and artificial flavors to imitate maple syrup. Real maple syrup is produced from maple tree sap.

So, how do you tell if maple syrup is fake? There are two ways. One is to look at the nutrition label. Is the main ingredient corn syrup? Does it have a long list of other ingredients and additives? If the answer to these questions are yes, then it's probably fake maple syrup. Real maple syrup will usually only list "maple syrup" as the ingredient.

A second way to tell if syrup is real or not is by putting it in a freezer. Real syrup will thicken but not freeze solid. Fake syrups typically freeze solid.

## Day 57:
1) 300 players
2) 63 points
3) 107 points
4) £40
5) 45 seconds
6) 96 feet long

## Day 58:

1) 10 inches
2) 4 times wider
3) 41 miles per hour
4) 1,680 miles shorter
5) 280 square miles
6) 7,064 square miles

Trivia) Zero. The Amazon River is over 4,000 miles long but does not have a single bridge crossing over it. There are few roads traveling through much of the Amazon Rainforest, so bridges aren't necessary. The width of the river also varies greatly during the rainy seasons and dry seasons, making bridge construction difficult.

## Day 59:

1) 23,158 homes
2) 221 cubic meters of water
3) 14 cubic meters of water
4) 27 fewer bags of grain
5) £576
6) £290

## Day 60:

1) 48 feet longer
2) 111 million krill
3) 2 cars
4) 10 days
5) 4 orcas
6) 16 dwarf sperm whales

Trivia) Did you know whales sing? Well, at least that's what people often call the long moans and cries that whales make–whale songs. Nobody knows for sure how far a whale's sounds can travel. The songs of humpback whales can be heard underwater thousands of miles away. Some people believe that their lower pitched sounds can travel over 10,000 miles underwater. If true, then a humpback on one side of the Pacific Ocean could be heard on the other side of the ocean.

## Day 61:

1) 48 years old
2) 140 miles per hour
3) £402
4) £300
5) £125
6) £142,800

## Day 62:

1) 27 pigeon eggs
2) 5 copper coins
3) 21 weeks
4) 13 pounds
5) 10 hours
6) 40 miles per hour faster

Trivia) Pigeons have been used in times of war for thousands of years. Hundreds of pigeons were used to send messages during WWI and WWII. Dozens of these pigeons were even awarded medals for their services.

Why give a pigeon a medal? Well, these pigeons risked their lives and were often injured while delivering their messages. Enemy soldiers tried to shoot pigeons down once they were released so that messages could not be delivered. Unfortunately, a lot of pigeons died this way.

Many messages were successfully delivered by pigeons. Sometimes, their messages were the only way for troops trapped behind enemy lines to communicate and send valuable information back to the main army. These messages saved the lives of countless soldiers.

## Day 63:

1) 411 people
2) £2,359
3) 55 people
4) 9:15 PM
5) £365
6) 690 miles

## Day 64:

1) 30 more pounds
2) 1,385 seeds
3) 10:26 AM
4) 2.5 mg more lycopene
5) 50 regular watermelons
6) £83,400

Trivia) It was a little over 350 pounds.

## Day 65:

1) 7 weeks
2) £13
3) £0.65
4) 1 hour and 31 minutes (91 minutes)
5) 4 times (Ralph will ride on the 5th time)
6) 8 times

## Day 66:

1) 8 cases
2) 229,593,000 people
3) 6 bites per hour
4) 180 days old
5) 15 seconds
6) 6 miles

Trivia) Male and female mosquitoes eat a lot of nectar. They travel from flower to flower to find nectar to eat, making mosquitoes great pollinators. While males only eat nectar, females occasionally crave a meal of blood too. They need nutrients from blood, such as proteins and iron, to grow and lay eggs.

## Day 67:

1) £448
2) 7 tour guides
3) £255
4) 120 square feet
5) 22 minutes per mile
6) 15 mountain goats

## Day 68:

1) 18,000 watts
2) 447 watts per hour
3) £7,480
4) 16 square meters
5) 11 years
6) £1,700

Trivia) The international space station has about 27,000 square feet of solar panels.

## Day 69:

1) £60
2) 41 fish
3) 336 pellets
4) 16 cages
5) 24 snakes
6) £41.51

## Day 70:

1) 5,400 times a minute
2) One and a half years (1.5 years)
3) 80 times
4) 40 inches longer
5) 75,000 people
6) £10,440

Trivia) See the next column →

# Answers

## Day 70: *Continued*

Trivia) A rattlesnake's rattle is what it uses to warn predators (and people) to not get too close. When the rattle breaks off, the snake will still shake its tail as a warning, but it will not be able to make a rattling noise. Even if a few rattles remain on the tail, the sound may not loud enough for people to hear when they are getting too close, resulting in unwanted snake bites.

## Day 71:

1) £85
2) 23 ticket machines
3) 3 hours and 30 minutes (3.5 hours)
4) 16 days
5) 170 km of track
6) £19,110

## Day 72:

1) 7 hours and 25 minutes
2) 3.29 meters
3) 6,200 years old
4) 7 hours and 30 minutes (7.5 hours)
5) 3 feet per second
6) 16,800 years older

Trivia) Mammoth Cave is located in the state of Kentucky. It is over 400 miles long and many experts believe the cave is likely longer. They believe there are more passages and chambers that still haven't been discovered.

## Day 73:

1) 65 feet
2) 280 miles per day
3) 27 barrels of water
4) 25 feet above deck
5) 245 gems
6) 42 gold coins each

## Day 74:

1) 20,000 kernels
2) 5 times
3) 36,000 pounds of corn a month
4) 3,905 million more bushels of corn
5) 5 bushels of corn
6) 9 candies

Trivia) Too much of any sugar, not just corn sweeteners, is considered to be bad for a person's health. Too much added sugars in a person's diet can increase the chances of developing certain diseases, such as type 2 diabetes and heart disease.

## Day 75:

1) 19 problems
2) 20 problems
3) 3 minutes per problem
4) 28 minutes
5) 15 mins and 5 seconds
6) 63 points

## Day 76:

1) 78,350 eggs
2) 4,240 trays of eggs
3) 31 eggs
4) 420 calories
5) 2,412 eggs
6) 13 dozen eggs

Trivia) It varies, but chickens often start laying eggs when they're about 18 weeks old.

# Answers

## Day 77:
1) £3,500 per month
2) 42,300 kg of garbage
3) 8 hours
4) 1,739 trash bins
5) 72 garbage trucks
6) 2,450 tons of garbage

## Day 78:
1) 400 pounds
2) 600 pounds of food
3) 7 adult gorillas
4) 422 words
5) 24 gorillas
6) 62 gorillas
Trivia) Gorillas and humans share about 98% of the same DNA. Only chimpanzees and bonobos have a closer genetic match to people.

## Day 79:
1) £3,775
2) £160
3) 111 paintings
4) 344 guests
5) £600 per day
6) 45 square meters

## Day 80:
1) 20,000 new species
2) At least 50 mL
3) 51 days
4) About 7 miles deep (6.86 miles)
5) 320,977,661 cubic miles more
6) 700 grams of salt
Trivia) The Amazon River is the world's largest river. It discharges about 55 million gallons of water every second. At this rate, it would take about 200,000 years for the Amazon River to refill the oceans' 321,000,000 cubic miles of space.

## Day 81:
1) 16 scuba divers
2) 425 scuba divers
3) 24 years old
4) 3 minutes and 34 seconds
5) 15 years (First convert cm to mm.)
6) 13 more minutes

## Day 82:
1) 6 times wider
2) 4,600 bugs a day
3) 341 bugs
4) 210 miles
5) 26 months
6) 27 Nymphs a day
Trivia) Some globe skimmers migrate from India to East Africa. To do this, they fly across the Indian ocean. Roundtrip, the migration distance is about 11,200 miles (18,000 km).

## Day 83:
1) 20 people
2) 4 scoops
3) £210
4) £57.15
5) 15 cupcakes
6) 13 people

## Day 84:
1) 1,907 cherries
2) 42 cherry trees
3) 2,025 kilograms
4) 10 tons
5) 16 feet
6) 63 pounds
Trivia) It's a variety of cherry specially bred for Canada's cool climates. Staccato cherry trees produce fruit many weeks later than most cherry tree species. This allows Canadian farmers to sell staccato cherry harvests well after the U.S. cherry season is over.

## Day 85:
1) 81 kg
2) £8,640
3) 39 minutes and 55 seconds
4) £8,750
5) £1,690
6) £5.75

## Day 86:
1) 677 more spines
2) 42 piglets
3) 166 hedgehogs
4) 33 grams each week
5) 630 kibbles
6) 25 nights
Trivia) A group of hedgehogs is called an "array."

## Day 87:
1) £462
2) 6 weeks
3) £69
4) 4 hours
5) 7 meatballs
6) 32 apple slices

## Day 88:
1) 33 feet longer
2) 2,150 times stronger (6,450x ÷ 3x = 2,150)
3) 27 times
4) 13 million light years away
5) 105mm
6) £3,600
Trivia) During Galileo's time, most people believed the sun revolved around the Earth. Galileo used his telescopes to study the stars and planets and realized the Earth revolved around the sun. He published his findings, proving that the Earth was not the center of the universe. The Catholic Church at the time believed the sun revolved around the Earth and had Galileo put on trial for publishing his findings as facts instead of hypotheses.

Galileo basically pleaded guilty to receive a lesser punishment, which was house arrest for the rest of his life. While under house arrest, he continued his scientific studies and published many more theories before he died. Today, many consider him to be the "father of modern science."

## Day 89:
1) £24
2) 10:33 AM
3) 3 hours and 45 minutes
4) £16 for each steak dinner
5) 112 customers
6) 452 to-go boxes

## Day 90:
1) 12 times longer
2) 15 hours
3) 2 pounds a year
4) 13,418 fewer tortoises
5) 163 years old
6) 49 items of fruit
Trivia) The oldest known tortoise was about 189 years old when the research for this book was taking place. This tortoise's name is Johnathan. Johnathan hatched in 1832.

Some other tortoises are claimed to be older than Johnathan, but it's difficult to prove their age. Records and documents of a tortoise's life are not always available, especially for tortoises that were born 200 or more years ago.

## Day 91:
1) 28,500 tires
2) 15 engines per hour
3) 1,150 automobiles a week
4) 306 employees
5) 385 four-seater cars
6) £8,311,000 a month

## Day 92:
1) 1%
2) 29%
3) 41 miles
4) 5 hours
5) 1,608,000 miles
6) 0.22 billion years old
Trivia) The oldest rocks on Earth are found near the Hudson Bay in Canada. Why haven't rocks that are 4.5 billion years old been found if that is how old Earth is? Well, Earth's crust is constantly recycled. Parts of the crust slowly slide back into the earth and becomes magma. New crust slowly forms in other places. Most rocks that existed over 4 billion years ago have long since been melted and no longer exist. Finding rocks that are 4.28 billion years old is incredibly rare.

## Day 93:
1) 35 employees
2) 1 minute and 35 seconds.
3) £460
4) 6 appointments per year
5) £35
6) £312

## Day 94:
1) 12,600 gallons of blood
2) 4 months
3) 1,000 times more
4) 48 lives
5) 5,355 people
6) 24 minutes
Trivia) There are about 0.2 milligrams of gold in a human body and most of it is located in the blood.

## Day 95:
1) 696 paintings
2) 180 more people (67 adults and 113 kids)
3) 179 students
4) 19,783 visitors
5) £93
6) £27,600

**Day 96:**

1) 60 miles per hour faster
2) 15 times slower
3) 1000 feet per minute
4) £720
5) 108 more pounds
6) £14.01

Trivia) During the making of this book, the current record for the highest parachute jump was about 135,900 feet above the ground. Alan Eustace performed the jump in 2014. Like the world's first parachute jump, Alan used a hydrogen balloon to carry him high above the Earth. In this case, the balloon took him near the top of the stratosphere. He fell for about 15 minutes and broke the speed of sound, which created a sonic boom that spectators on the ground were able to hear.

**Day 97:**

1) 423 people
2) £127
3) 5 days
4) £5,180
5) £1,113 more
6) 762 feet

**Day 98:**

1) 39 minutes
2) 75 eggs
3) 17 tarantula tanks
4) 34 years old
5) £7.47
6) 13 crickets

Trivia) The goliath bird-eating tarantula is the largest tarantula species. Its leg span can be 11 inches wide (28 cm). It's also the heaviest spider species in the world.

**Day 99:**

1) 152 animals
2) 10 more dogs
3) 8 sacks of food
4) 27 walks
5) £1,534
6) £828 each month

**Day 100:**

1) 401,337 jellies
2) 4 times longer
3) 117 pounds heavier
4) 2,067,161 cnidocytes
5) 17 minutes
6) 2 mL

Trivia) The Irukandji jellyfish is believed to be the smallest jellyfish. It's only 2 cm wide. Despite its small size, its sting is extremely painful and sometimes deadly. Irukandji jellyfish usually send dozens of people to the hospital each year.

*Thank you moms, dads, and caregivers.*
*Thank you teachers and homeschooling parents.*
*Special thanks to all the helpful big brothers and sisters.*
*Ultimate thanks to the student. It's your effort that matters most!*

**Have questions, suggestions, or ideas for future resources?**
**Contact us at** www.HumbleMath.com



ISBN: 978-1-63578-345-2 (UK Edition)

Current contact information for Humble Math can be found at www.HumbleMath.com
Current contact information for Libro Studio LLC can be found at www.LibroStudioLLC.com

Image Credits:
John D Sirlin/Shutterstock.com (Cover, Day 2)
Melanie DeFazio/Shutterstock.com (Day 4)
Brian Lasenby/Shutterstock.com (Day 6)
cobalt88/Shutterstock.com (Day 6)
Humble Math Contributor (Cover, Title Page, Days 6, 8, 10, 16, 20, 22, 28, 32, 34, 38, 40, 44, 56, 64, 68, 74, 80, 84, 88)
Valentyn Volkov/Shutterstock.com (Cover, Day 10)
Macrovector/Shutterstock.com (Days 14, 24, 94)
AKaiser/Shutterstock.com (Cover, Title Page, Day 18)
Hennadii H/Shutterstock.com (Days 30, 62, 76)
Drp8/Shutterstock.com (Day 36)
youli zhao/Shutterstock.com (Title Page, Day 46)
Bjoern Wylezich/Shutterstock.com (Cover, Day 48)
Zonda/Shutterstock.com (Cover, Days 50, 68, 88)
ruek66/Shutterstock.com (Day 54)
BlueRingMedia/Shutterstock.com (Title Page, Days 12, 26, 100)
Alexander Demyanenko/Shutterstock.com (Title Page, Day 42)
Korvil/Shutterstock.com (Day 52)
Anna L. e Marina Durante/Shutterstock.com (Day 52)
Dr Morley Read/Shutterstock.com (Day 58)
A7880S/Shutterstock.com (Day 60)
Carboxylase/Shutterstock.com (Day 60)
Dieter Hawlan/Shutterstock.com (Day 66)
Dmitrijs Bindemanis/Shutterstock.com (Day 66)
Audrey Snider-Bell/Shutterstock.com (Day 70)
IrinaK/Shutterstock.com (Day 72)
SARAWUTK/Shutterstock.com (Day 74)
Krakenimages.com/Shutterstock.com (Cover, Day 78)
Mr. SUTTIPON YAKHAM/Shutterstock.com (Days 82, 86, 90, 98)
Apple Art/Shutterstock.com (Day 92)
Seahorse Vector/Shutterstock.com (Title Page, Day 96)

Printed in Great Britain
by Amazon

87082869R00066